COMMA
SENSE

Also by John Shore

Penguins, Pain, & the Whole Shebang

Also by Richard Lederer

Adventures of a Verbivore
Anguished English
Basic Verbal Skills (with Phillip Burnham)
The Bride of Anguished English
The Circus of Words
Crazy English
The Cunning Linguist
Fractured English
Get Thee to a Punnery
The Giant Book of Animal Jokes (with James Ertner)
Have a Punny Christmas
Literary Trivia (with Michael Gilleland)
A Man of My Words
The Miracle of Language
More Anguished English
The Play of Words
Pun & Games
Puns Spooken Here
The Revenge of Anguished English
Sleeping Dogs Don't Lay (with Richard Dowis)
The Word Circus
Word Play Crosswords, volumes 1 and 2 (with Gayle Dean)
The Write Way (with Richard Dowis)

COMMA SENSE

A FUNdamental Guide to Punctuation

RICHARD LEDERER
AND JOHN SHORE

Illustrations by James McLean

ST. MARTIN'S PRESS ❅ NEW YORK

Design by Phil Mazzone

ISBN 0-7394-6503-1

CONTENTS

INTRODUCTION
ON YOUR MARKS!

’[ ],:_…!-( ).?“”;

One of life's great oddities is how it's filled with things that don't seem as if they belong together, yet are inextricably joined. Weddings, for instance, and clothes you can barely breathe in. Neckties and having a job. King Kong and Fay Wray. Airplanes and air. Sweet deliciousness and cavities. Bovine flatulence and ozone depletion. Lamb and mint jelly. Koala bears and weirdly humongous claws. Banana slugs and a rational universe. Menopause and a rational universe. Bill Gates and the future of the universe.

Foremost among things in the world that shouldn't go together but do are Understanding Punctuation and Accruing Personal Power. But it's as true as true gets: If you don't understand punctuation, you can't write right. And if you can't write right, you can't positively influence so much of what's critical to your life.

It's a fact: Good punctuation makes for a good life.

Sure, it seems unfair. But so do lots of things. Parking meters, for instance, seem very unfair. But you can rail against them until Lovely Rita the Meter Maid finally calls for backup—and you'll still end up with a ticket every time you forget to leave the house without a roll of quarters.

Like it or not, writing well—not artistically, not ornately, not floridly, but just competently—really is the difference between being largely able to define your own life and having much of your life defined for you. Writing is, in a word, power. And trying to write a Post-it note—much less anything of any substance—without understanding punctuation is like trying to build a house without nails: It'll look awful, and no one will want to come near it.

Think it's going too far to say that punctuation is the difference between control and chaos, between justice and injustice, between true inner peace and false outer agony? Think that sounds a tad dramatic? Really? Have you ever had the paint on your new car start peeling off in huge flakes? Ever had a rabid boss ruin your life? Ever yearned for someone of the opposite sex to fall heels over head in love with you?

You see the point: If you want to impress that special gal or fella, use your blotchy new car to run over your rabid boss.

No, the *real* point is: Knowing how to write clear, succinct, and, if need be, charming letters, notes, and e-mails is one extremely dependable way to persuade people to start thinking about matters in precisely the way you would prefer them to.

It's how you get your car repainted for free. It's how you (eventually) get your loser boss fired. It's how you get that gal or fella to lie awake nights wondering why they never learned how to punctuate, so that they could scribe communiqués as enticing as yours.

Just look at the difference between these two love notes:

My Dear Pat,

The dinner we shared the other night—it was absolutely lovely! Not in my wildest dreams could I ever imagine anyone as perfect as you are. Could you—if only for a moment—think of our being together forever? What a cruel joke to have you come into my life only to leave again; it would be heaven denied. The possibility of seeing you again makes me giddy with joy. I face the time we are apart with great sadness.

John

P.S.: *I would like to tell you that I love you. I can't stop thinking that you are one of the prettiest women on earth.*

My Dear,

Pat the dinner we shared the other night. It was absolutely lovely—not! In my wildest dreams, could I ever imagine anyone? As perfect as you are, could you—if only for a moment—think? Of our being together forever: what a cruel joke! To have you come into my life only to leave again: it would be heaven! Denied the possibility of seeing you again makes me giddy. With joy I face the time we are apart.

With great "sadness,"

John

P.S.: *I would like to tell you that I love you. I can't. Stop thinking that you are one of the prettiest women on earth.*

You see the difference punctuation makes? The first letter is a clear (albeit clunky) profession of undying affection; the second is sure to sweep Pat *onto* her feet. The only thing separating one document from the other is, of course, punctuation.

Never forget: Punctuation can mean the difference between a second date and a restraining order.

The problem with punctuation is threefold: Its rules are seemingly arbitrary; it's boring; and no one knows how to do it. But these three objections to punctuation combined pale in magnitude next to the single Great Truth about it: If you fail to master punctuation, your life will be littered with the shards of broken dreams. Or, less melodramatically, your life will be littered with the shards of broken beer bottles, the contents of which you have drunk to avoid thinking about your dead-end job.

As a step toward your not ever having to step on those broken beer bottles, let us consider the reasonable reasons for which, we know, you might have already put this book down, and moved on to something that doesn't involve a potential brain sprain.

The rules of punctuation seem arbitrary. How can they not, when an apostrophe looks like nothing in this world so much as a comma that can't keep its feet on the ground? Or when, by simply placing next to that wafting comma its twin, one creates (of all things) a quotation mark? And who—oh, *who*?—can figure out what's supposed to happen when it's time to use a comma within—or is it outside?—a quotation mark? The prospect of trying to wrangle the two in order impels most of us to pick up the phone immediately and call the person we were thinking of writing.

Sometimes single quotation marks are correct. Sometimes the standard double does the trick. Sometimes *both* are in order. (And sometimes—for we might as well say now what we'll certainly be hollering later—quotation marks are an absolute crime against humanity.)

A semicolon is like a comma—only different. A semicolon

is also like a colon—only it's actually less like a colon than it is like a comma. (A semicomma, we should note, doesn't exist; we just made the word up. But it sounds like a punctuation mark that should exist, doesn't it?)

Periods are used in abbreviations. They also, of course, mark the end of a sentence. But if a sentence ends with an abbreviation, what then?

Hyphens transform two words into (sort of) one word. In that sense they help make words more user-friendly. Or is it user friendly?

Adding an apostrophe and *s* makes a singular noun possessive: *The dog* becomes *the dog's*. But what if the noun already ends in *s*—or, worse, what if it's a *plural* noun that ends in *s*?

Kids menu? Kid's menu? Kids' menu? Kids's menu?

Before we all run amok, let us now state that the rules for punctuation only *seem* arbitrary. Rest assured that they are not. Everything in the universe must obey certain specific rules, and punctuation is no different. We have made it our business to ensure that you master those rules—which, like all sets of rules, only seem complicated until you become familiar with them.

Punctuation is obscure and boring. "Use commas to set off parenthetical words, conjunctive adverbs, nouns of direct address, nonrestrictive appositives, phrases, and dependent clauses." See what we mean? We, your faithful punctuation guys, believe that punctuation doesn't have to be obscure and boring. We know that because we've had such a blast writing this book and trying to make the rules sprightly and accessible.

No one knows how to do it. Well, not *no* one. Some people really understand punctuation. Unfortunately, they tend to be the kind of people who, when you're at a party reaching the very pinnacle of your joke, interject with, "You mean different *from,* not different *than,*" or, "It's *whom,* not *who.*" But normal people—the sort who actually get invited to parties more than once—aren't particularly punctilious about being pontificating punctuation pundits.

Language experts agree that one of the primary reasons people so often associate commas with comas is that computers have somehow driven a wedge between the "Think/Take Care/Don't Embarrass Your Mother" part of everyone's brain and the "Freakin' GO For It, dude!!" part. Study after study supports the notion that there's something about cyberspace that compels people to just float about, willy-nilly, free from the restraints of Careful Punctuation that once kept us all so grounded. Young people today find a lesson on punctuation as painful as speaking a sentence that doesn't have the word *like* in it. They don't read or write essays. They don't write letters, or stories, or . . . travelogues. They don't even write *words.* They *text-message.* They text-message *a lot.* And to say that messages delivered via cell-phone "text" tend to lack punctuation is like saying that yaks tend to be hairy, or that professional basketball players tend to be tall.

Take, for instance, this transcript of a typical text-message "conversation" between two teenagers, Sam and Pam (whose names have been changed to protect us from having to type too much):

SAM: r u ok
PAM: ya u
SAM: no
PAM: y
SAM: sik
PAM: o
SAM: u

PAM: no

SAM: o

PAM: flgheoighihaahg

SAM: aqqssgooghehbnser

PAM: lier

SAM: xblgh2 iipw

PAM: bhggkittld

SAM: ghsjgl2 liytqcv00

PAM: lier

SAM: vvvvvvv

PAM: hmmmmm

SAM: do

PAM: ok

SAM: ffp

PAM: by

SAM: fxgyrtosoekgisllgkghsj

PAM: o stop

This typical teenage exchange makes clear why so many education and language experts are sounding the alarm. The dialogue squeaks like chalk over the blackboard of adult sensibilities—and helps explain why so many grown-ups believe that today's teenagers communicate primarily through telepathy.

Why so few of the rest of us properly punctuate remains a bit of a mystery. One theory has it that in the mid-1960s U.S. schools quit teaching punctuation to allow for more time spent teaching children how to tie-dye T-shirts and sing hippie songs. Another maintains that our brains are simply overloaded from Input Glut. If we're going to keep track of the contestants on *American Idol,* for instance, then something's gotta give.

Hello, ninety-minute informercial; good-bye, "Use commas to set off introductory appositives, phrases, and dependent clauses."

Whatever the reason, the fact is that the average person can't punctuate their way out of "See Spot run." Lost in a sea of punctuational possibilities, they come up with "See? Spot run!" or "See Spot! Run!" or "See, Spot has the runs!" This doesn't make them bad people, of course, or spectacularly dense people, or anything like that. It makes them people who don't know how to punctuate. That there are so many of them out there is absolutely wonderful news for you: It means that people who *can* punctuate stand out like Thinking Gods.

Thinking Gods!

You want to stand out like that, don't you? You want your written messages to carry real weight: to persuade, scare, charm, defend, or offend people to exactly the degree you desire, don't you?

Of course you do.

You want what we all want: More Power.

And there are few better ways, if any, to acquire more power in one fell swoosh than to master the fundamentals of punctuation. Believe it now, or believe it when you find a bunch of people standing around the water cooler at work laughing at one of your memos. (The cruel fact about punctuation, remember, is that a person doesn't have to know how to use it in order to know, right away, when someone *else* has botched it beyond respectability.)

"Your report, Ms. Jones, was dismal; I cannot imagine how you ever came to work here." That's power. "Your report Ms. Jones was dismal I cannot imagine. how you ever came to work here?" is . . . so not.

The power's in the punctuation, baby. And we're gonna show you how to be a power pack of punctuational potency.

Here's how we've laid out the rest of our book:

We'll first present the punctuation marks that end sentences—the Period, Question Mark, and Exclamation Point. Next will come those marks that separate the parts of a sentence—the Comma and the Semicolon. These are followed by introducers—the Colon and the Dash. Finally, we take a look at the rest of the marks of good writing, roughly in order of how frequently they appear—the Apostrophe, Quotation Marks, Parentheses and Brackets, the Hyphen, and the Ellipsis. As a kind of Super Index, we'll top the book off with a "Cheat Sheet," a quickie overview of all the marks in alphabetical order.

At the beginning of each chapter, you'll see a giant version of The Next Mark to Conquer. Early in each chapter, in **bold-face,** you'll encounter the down-and-dirty, no-frills, prof-proof, principal principle for each mark. Beneath that we'll explain and show that rule in action. We'll make sure you get it, and won't forget it. Then we'll **boldly face** additional less-vital-but-things-you-still-need-to-sear-into-your-brain guide-lines for each mark.

We think that when you're done with this book, you'll be well on your way to becoming one succinct, articulate, intimi-dating dude or dudette.

Or, you know: just a normal person who writes well.

CHAPTER 1
THE PERIOD

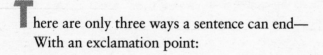

There are only three ways a sentence can end—
With an exclamation point:

   You won!

With a question mark:

   You won?

Or with a period:

   I know you won, but I'm having trouble believing it.

That's it. Those are your choices. Every sentence that's not an exclamation or a question must end with a period. And because people are by and large too proud to ask too many questions and too shy to go around hollering all the time, the vast (not the half-vast) majority of sentences are what are called declarative statements—statements that just say something and therefore end in a period.

It is difficult to think of any other instance in life in which something as small as the period carries so much clout. It's a mark so dinky that farsighted fleas court it. Yet virtually any declarative statement—a picturesque description, a mild directive, a thoughtful observation, or a wandering exposition that starts out as if it's going somewhere specific but about halfway through makes clear enough that if it ever *does* pull in anywhere, it'll do so carrying the corpses of whatever readers were unlucky enough to have climbed aboard it in the first place—must stop whenever the period says it's time.

Verily is the period the crosswalk guard of our language.

If only there were any famous crosswalk guards, we could use one of them right here as a metaphor for the period. But, of course, most of us never give a thought to those stalwart sedan stoppers except when we're watching them from inside our cars, feeling weird about how much we, too, want to wear a cop's hat and a bright orange vest and hold up a big sign stopping all the cars so little kids can be on their scholarly little way.

That's why we resist making crosswalk guards famous: It ticks us off that they have better jobs than we do. Why should they get any more glory? They've got their hats, their signs, their cool sashes, their *white gloves*. That's enough. Any more, and they'll feel empowered enough to start shooting out our tires to stop us.

No, as a metaphor for the period the crosswalk guard won't do at all.

We need someone small. Someone powerful. Someone who at first seemed to have no potential. Someone with attitude. Someone with finishing power.

We need *Seabiscuit*!

He's small: Sizewise, Seabiscuit was closer to a merry-go-round horse than a stakes-hogging racehorse.

He's powerful: In a much-ballyhooed match race, Seabiscuit spotted the stately War Admiral whole hands and still whipped him.

Even equine experts didn't think that the plucky little horse had any potential: There was a time when Seabiscuit couldn't be given away. (Just as, in the beginning, no one thought the period would be able to reach the finish line, let alone stop the most puffed up of sentences. The giant, imposing question mark was supposed to be the punctuation leader—and you see how *that* turned out.)

He's got attitude: Seabiscuit liked to torment his fellow racehorses by always *just* beating them. (Just as the period seems to enjoy taunting letters and words by letting them think they *might* have a chance of ending up ahead of it. It's wrong to behave that way, of course—but sometimes that's the kind of attitude that makes a winner a winner.)

He's got finishing power. Seabiscuit surged to the finish line first in an awesomely high percentage of his races.

And finally, just as Seabiscuit needed a strong and thoughtful rider in order to do his best (Johnny "Red" Pollard and 'Biscuit had a special bond), so the period needs a strong and thoughtful writer to do its best. And that writer is you, friend. So get that foot up in that stirrup, swing that other leg up and over, and let's show these whippersnapper words how the little boys do it.

- **A period marks the conclusion of any sentence that doesn't end with an exclamation point or a question mark:**

  Singing with utmost exuberance and abandon and filling in the music-only parts with dance steps reminiscent of how impossible it was to even walk in disco shoes, Bert delivered a karaoke version of K.C. and the Sunshine Band's "Get Down Tonight" that was a testimony to what it was about disco in the first place that compelled so many of us to drop out of high school.

  Today Einstein's brain is stored in formaldehyde in a jar, in the hopes that future scientists will be able to figure out what exactly they're supposed to do with a brain in a jar.

- **In U.S. punctuation, periods always—and we do mean always—go inside quotation marks.**

  They do things backwards in Britain, like driving on the wrong side of the road and serving warm beer and cold toast. But the Brits' system of placing the period outside quotation marks actually makes more sense. Still, we live in the U.S. of A., so we'll say it again:

- **In U.S. punctuation, periods always—and we do mean always—go inside quotation marks:**

  "What I remember," said Carl as he lay upon his psychotherapist's couch being suddenly filled with early childhood memories, "is sitting in the middle of the floor of our old family room, wearing those white, plastic, over-the-diaper panty things. It was *mortifying* to have to sit around all day, looking like the fuse on a whipped cream bomb."

● **Periods belong inside parentheses that enclose a free-standing sentence and outside parentheses that enclose material that is not a full statement:**

The new album by the band Bob's Pock Mark is absolutely superb (bearing in mind, of course, that none of the band's members can sing or play any instruments). The guys in the band say that they're proud of songs such as "Love Backwards Is Evolve, Almost" and "Feed Me" because they're socially galvanizing, radically artistic messages. (They can be also be played on a haircomb.)

● **Periods are also used with numbers, abbreviations, and initials:**

1. Mr. E. Z. Rider
2. Ms. Q. T. Pie
3. Dr. M. T. Handed
4. Prof. I. V. Leaguer, Ph.D.

There. That's it. You're done. You now know everything there is to know about the period. Period. End of sentence.

CHAPTER 2
THE QUESTION MARK

There's no question but that asking questions throughout human history is how we, as a race, have made it to where we are today. There's virtually nothing in our lives that we now take for granted that didn't begin with someone somewhere asking a critical question. What would life be like today if no one had ever dared to ask such questions as:

"Why don't we try *pointed* sticks?"

"Wouldn't wearing something along the lines of what the animals wear be better than coating ourselves with mud every morning?"

"I wonder if we couldn't come up with better protection from the elements than just holding boulders over our heads wherever we go?"

"I wonder if what dropped out of that chicken just now is edible?"

"I wonder if the wheel would work better if we made it into a shape other than square?"

"Hey, has anyone else noticed that there's only one horrible despot, and about a *million* of us?"

So there it is: Without the power of the question, it's clear that today we'd all be running around covered in mud, ruled by an evil despot, and struggling to hold boulders over our heads while poking our enemies and our potential meals with a blunt stick. And we'd never have been able to ride in an SUV.

From the dawn of civilization humans have certainly benefited from inquiring minds that wanted to know. But no one has asked more life-altering questions than the great Albert Einstein, destined to be forever revered as the intuitive genius who gazed deep and hard into the dark stillness of the celestial abode and dared to ask: "What is the deal with my hair? Why do I always look as if I'd just been struck by lightning? When—oh *when*?—is someone going to invent conditioner?"

We jest, of course. As anyone who has ever seen a picture of him knows, Einstein couldn't have cared less about his hair. He knew it protected his head—and that was good enough for him. Because inside that head were percolating answers to the kinds of questions that only Einstein could ask—and that only he could answer.

Before Einstein published his monumental, paradigm-smashing Special Theory of Relativity in 1905, we believed that time and space were fixed, firmly and eternally rooted in mathematical truths established two centuries earlier by another physics genius with dramatic hair, Sir Isaac Newton. (Newton's wiggy hair protected him against a bushel of apples that, from time to time, was known to bounce off his skull.)

Before Einstein, time and space were absolutes. After Einstein, they became, well, relative. (And the picnic was pretty much over for matter, energy, and gravity, too.)

Ultimately, Einstein was able to boil down his discovery

about the true relationship between energy and mass (namely, that they're different forms of the same thing) to his famous equation, $e = mc^2$—which is, without a doubt, the most succinct expression of anything in any language ever. As just about everyone knows, in this equation, e stands for energy, m represents mass, and c^2 is the square of the speed of light.

In other words, to find out how much energy would be in a thing if it were suddenly transformed into *pure* energy, all you have to do is multiply its weight by the square of the speed of light.

Isn't it funny how something can become so *obvious* once someone else points it out? It's like looking at a paper clip: Of *course* it would work! Of *course* $e = mc^2$! Of *course* if the speed of light is constant, then time and distance must be relative!

Duh.

Doesn't it drive you crazy that *you* didn't see it first? Us, too. But, whaddaya gonna do? Now Einstein's famous, and all that's left for us to do is try to figure out how the legacy of his genius is supposed to provide us with the answers to math test questions such as:

Two men are sitting in window seats in two different trains hurtling in opposite directions. One man is wearing a watch; the other is wearing a hat. When train A leaves the station, the time is exactly twelve noon. When train B leaves its station, the time is twelve midnight. The man aboard train A knows what time it is, because he is the man with the watch. The man aboard train B isn't sure of the exact time, but he knows it's somewhere near midnight, because when dining on bratwurst about an hour before, he asked a woman what time it was, and she said eleven.

At the moment the two trains pass one another, train A is going 100 miles per hour, and train B is traveling at twice the speed of light. Now imagine that both trains freeze at the very moment the two windows at which the men are sitting are directly across from each another. When the man with the watch looks over at the man with the hat, which of the following will he see?:

(a)   A child in a hat much too large for him;

(b)   A man pasted against the back of his chair wearing that bug-eyed, teeth-bared, Quasimodo-nostriled, flappy-cheeked expression people get when they go superfast;

(c)   An empty train seat;

(d)   Waldo.

See? Einstein's *theories* are simple—but *applying* them is a can of wormholes. Well, no matter. Because ultimately it's less important to be able to answer a question than it is to ask one in the first place. And when you *write* a question, there's only one rule about the question mark you need to bear in mind:

? Put one at the end of a question:

Was Einstein such a science maverick because his own last name violates the "*i*-before-*e*-except-after-*c*" rule twice?

Einstein's hair looked like that because he asked himself, "What would happen if I stuck my finger into a wall socket?"

Did Einstein really say, "My hair is definitely better this way"? [Note that in the "wall socket" example, Einstein's words are actually the question—so the question mark goes inside the quotation marks. In the example after that, the sentence itself is a question, not Einstein's quotation, so the question mark goes *outside* the quotation marks.]

Did you know that Albert Einstein played linebacker for the Princeton University football team?

Place a question mark at the end of a question. Now *that's* easy. There's no reason at all why that simple formula—unlike Einstein's simple formula—should ever become a matter of gravity.

CHAPTER 3
THE EXCLAMATION POINT

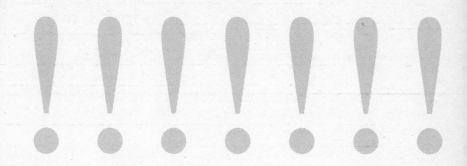

The exclamation point is perfectly named: You can just *tell* what it does. The names of the other marks reveal nothing about their purpose: *Ellipsis* sounds like a medical term for a muscular dysfunction of the lips. One might guess *parentheses* to be some sort of hypothetical proposal presented by a mom or dad ("A Parent's Thesis on the Matrix of Dynamics Supporting the Validity of the Imperative 'Because I Said So' "). *Comma* is dangerously close to *coma*. *Apostrophe* ("a pa's trophy") sounds like a father's reward for winning a golf tournament. *Hyphens* sound dauntingly as though you need to scale a "high fence" to master them.

And what else can the word *semicolon* refer to but a truck parked on someone's rear end? Either that, or someone with only . . . well, never mind.

But *exclamation point*! It removes all mystery! This one has a point to make. And—true to its very nature—it's not wasting any time making it. Once we know the name of this mark, we have a very strong sense of its function. **Use the exclamation point to emphasize an emotion or put backbone into a command.**

But that's not really enough for us, is it? We wouldn't want to be known or understood solely on the basis of how we function, would we? We don't want to be defined by what we *do*; we all want to be defined by who we *are*.

So who, really, *is* this inciter of excitement, this titan of tingle, this prince of palpitation? If we delved inside this flashiest of points, whom, exactly, would we find there?

In order to discover the inner exclamation point, we must, of course, deeply and truly identify with it. Like actors trying to grasp the essence of a character they mean to play, we must *become* the exclamation point if we are really going to know it at all.

So here's what you do: Go stand in front of a mirror. Look into the other side of the glass and try to evince in your expression the intent, purpose, and entire *being* of the exclamation point. *Feel* its surprise; its natural ebullience; its spontaneous emotional urgency. Become one with the exclamation point.

Go ahead. Make the face of the exclamation point.

Now quick: Whom do you look like?

That's right: Lucy Ricardo.

And there you have it: *Lucy is the exclamation point!*

Okay, stop making that face now. You might strain something.

All you need do is delve into the inner core of the exclamation point, and the person you'll find there is none other than film comedienne and television megastar Lucille Ball, also known as Lucy Ricardo—her bright red hair, her dress with the huge polka dots, her irrepressible, over-the-top energy.

Bearing Lucy in mind—and, for that matter, the whole cast of the *I Love Lucy* show—let's take a look at the variety of emotions whose expressions can be enhanced through the use of the exclamation point:

Anger:

Luuuucy! You got some 'splainin' to do!

Stop complaining, Ethel! You ought to be grateful that when you married me, you acquired the name Mertz!

Oh, Fred, stop being so cheap—and stop wearing your pants up around your neck!

Surprise:

Ricky's gonna let me sing at the club!

What! You're having another baby! But we sleep in separate beds! Now you really got some 'splainin' to do!

Lucy, Danny Thomas is in your kitchen! Again!

Love:

I love you, Ricky!

I love you, Lucy!

I love you, Ethel!

I love Lucy, Fred!

Pride:

I run the best nightclub in the city!

I've got the reddest hair in this building!

I married a woman much younger than I!

I still haven't murdered Fred in his sleep!

Desperation:

They're closing my nightclub!

Howdy Doody moved into 3-G! Now I don't have the reddest hair in the building!

Even though Ethel's pretty young, she dresses like a frumpy grandmother!

I still haven't murdered Fred in his sleep!

Joy:

It's a boy! We're gonna give him an inferiority complex for life by calling him Little Ricky!

Oh, Fred! Ricky bought Lucy a new car, a new washing machine, and all new bedroom furniture!

Oh, Ethel! We're about to get an old car, an old washing machine, and some old bedroom furniture!

And so on. There's really no emotion whose written expression can't be enhanced by the exclamation mark. Do beware, however, of using this punchy point too often. Remember the boy who cried wolf. You can't get people excited about something if you're excited about everything. And, please, never use two or more exclamation points in a clump!!! That's too much like shouting. Like TYPING EVERYTHING IN CAPITAL LETTERS IN AN E-MAIL MESSAGE.

So with the exclamation point—as, indeed, with any mark of punctuation—remember how important it is to be always on the ball.

CHAPTER 4
THE COMMA

The comma is the Allan Pinkerton of punctuation marks.

What? You don't know who Allan Pinkerton is? Well, in 1861, at the request of understandably jittery, newly elected President Abraham Lincoln, Pinkerton founded the Secret Service. And he got that assignment because, eleven years earlier in Chicago, he'd opened the Pinkerton Detective Agency, rendering himself American's first private eye. The slogan of his new business was "The All-Seeing Eye," and the logo was an image of a single open eye with the words "We Never Sleep." Hence the development, over time, of the term *private eye*— deriving from that eye image and coupled with the fact that . . . um . . . people who never sleep tend to look pretty awful, and so require a lot of privacy.

Allan Pinkerton was America's first Smart, Sneaky Guy Who Kept Order. Maintaining a low profile, this prototypical plainclothesman/detective/spy worked mightily before, throughout, and after the Civil War to ferret out the nefarious doings of American ne'er-do-wells, scalawags, and putzes who, for their own ends, sought to upset the Official Order of Things, which Pinkerton was dedicated to preserving. If you went afoul of the law, you'd have to answer, sooner or later, to someone from the Pinkerton Detective Agency.

Well, the comma is just like that—low profile, diligent, dedicated to maintaining order, amenable to creative improvisation, always working just below the surface to keep things in order and the cogwheels of society turning. Like Pinkerton's men, commas are ubiquitous, which is a big word meaning that they're all over the place; you see more commas than any other punctuation mark. When we're writing, and things begin to go awry, what do we most often turn to in order to set them straight again? You got it: that ubiquitous little squiggle, the comma.

Come to think of it, wouldn't the *pinkerton* be a better name for the comma? The thing *looks* like a "pinkerton," doesn't it? *Comma* is just so close to *coma,* which is what most of us tend to slide into whenever we have to really think about the comma. Why tempt fate that way? *Pinkerton* is something a person could stay interested in.

When you write, rather than speak, you need punctuation marks to serve your readers in the same way that timing, pitch, and inflection serve your listeners. The primary purpose of the comma is to make reading easier by establishing relationships between and among the parts of your written statements.

What's the difference between a cat and a comma?

A cat has claws at the end of its paws—but (har! har!) a comma is a pause at the end of a clause.

The most important function of the comma is to indicate a natural pause. If you use commas in that way, without bothering consciously to follow the gazillion rules we'll soon be laying on you, you will not be wrong often.

We urge you to rely on your own interior sensibilities to tell you how or if to use a comma. Just ask yourself if a comma *sounds* better in the place you're considering using one. That's an instinct you can have real faith in. Because as technically dense as explications about commas can become, the absolute bottom line is that if you can talk, and if you can listen to the way *other* people talk, then you're perfectly capable of understanding the precise role commas are meant to play in the written word.

When you listen to people talk, what you'll hear are lots and lots of *pauses*. Pauses are so critical to human communication it's virtually impossible to communicate clearly and effectively without them. It simply can't be done. If you try you'll end up sounding like an irritating monotonous cretin with some sort of profoundly alienating cerebral malfunction that won't allow you to talk or write like a normal person but instead causes you to drone on and on without ever pausing to let anyone catch his breath or in any way prepare for what you might want to say following whatever you just said which if you don't seek help for and fix you'll discover is a problem and sooner than you might think you'll be dragged out into an alley somewhere beaten up and left in a Dumpster you poor pause challenged person.

That's the core, fundamental, and irreducible truth of the ever-accommodating comma: Commas are meant to make readers pause and collect themselves a little before they move on. That's their purpose in life, and that's what they're doing every single time you ever see one.

So, when in doubt about a sentence, read it aloud. Notice where you naturally find yourself pausing—where, in effect, you *must* pause. Chances are that'll be a good place for a comma.

Your understanding this principle allows us to open the door and pull out the big guns; that is, to now lay out the suc- cinct, no-nonsense, grammar-teachers-will-love-this-part Actual Comma Rules. Think of the following as your supertight, handy-dandy, one-stop shop for all your comma rules. Whether you strew commas through your sentences like confetti or plant them like precious seeds, singly and far apart from each other, a little time spent learning the accepted conventions may eliminate comma trauma from your life.

Use commas to separate words, phrases, or clauses in a series. A series, by the way, is a succession of two or more items cast in similar grammatical form. A series can consist of nouns:

> The secret recipe for the superdelicious drink I invented includes vodka, grapefruit juice, raspberries, a splash of rye, and ketchup.

> Before leaving for his nightly crime spree, Simon checked to make sure he had a flashlight, a length of rope, gloves, a grappling hook, pliers, a skeleton key, a coat hanger, an energy bar, and a tube of Shimmering Pink lipstick.

A series can string together a sequence of verbs:

> The Frisbee sailed silently through the air, bounced off the kitchen wall, and splashed down in my chicken soup.

A series can be a succession of adjectives:

> My red, white, and blue rubber ducky is my favorite bath toy.

A series can be made up of clauses:

> I came, I saw the uncut grass, and I ran back into the house.

Note that we have placed commas before each of the con-junctions (in the examples above, the word *and*) that precede the last item in each series. This little mark is called the serial comma. Most newspapers and many other publications don't employ this serial comma, but in more formal writing, such as essays, business letters, and literary works (like this highbrow book), the serial comma is ordinarily retained. We recommend the use of the serial comma because we have found that in many sentences the comma before the conjunction is an aid to clarity, emphasis, and meaning. Consider:

For dinner, the Girl Scouts ate steak, onions and ice cream. [It sounds as if the Scouts devoured a yucky concoc-tion of onions and (urp!) ice cream.]

For dinner, the Girl Scouts ate steak, onions, and ice cream. [The serial comma in this sentence avoids such gas-tronomic ambiguity.]

The serial comma is an aid to clarity, emphasis and mean-ing. [Here, the rhythm of the series sounds uneven.]

The serial comma is an aid to clarity, emphasis, and meaning. [Notice how the serial comma helps the final term, *meaning,* to ring out as loudly as the others.]

At summer camp I missed my dog, my little brother, the odor of my dad's pipe and my boyfriend. [This sentence mis-speaks for itself.]

Finally, note the havoc wreaked by the absence of the serial comma in the following, reputedly real-life book dedication:

> To my parents, the Pope and Mother Teresa

Use commas to list adjectives in a series if the adjectives are of equal importance.

If you could place the word *and* between each adjective, use commas:

> They live in a large, comfortable, well-designed house.

Do not use commas to list adjectives in a series if the adjectives seem so closely related as to form a single unit:

> They live in a large two-story country house. [no commas because there are no understood *and*s here]

Use commas before coordinating conjunctions to join two independent clauses.

We live in a universe in which people, creatures, and objects do things. The doer is usually the subject of a statement, the action is the verb: In *I sing thrillingly, I* is the subject, and *sing* is the verb. In *He sucks eggs, He* is the subject, and *sucks* is the verb. A group of words containing a subject and a verb makes a clause.

An *independent* clause is a collection of words that, if called upon to do so, *could* exist alone as a sentence. If, in the course of the words appearing upon the page, these self-contained units of verbiage had happened to find themselves all alone, without any dependent clauses yapping at their heels or leaning on them for support, they would be just fine.

Independent clauses don't need anything beyond what they show up with, man. They're set. They're strong. They're ready to rock.

Independent clauses are the Green Berets of the sentence.

Take, for instance, the following sentence, which consists of nothing more (or less) than a single independent clause, which in Comp. 101 is known as a **simple sentence:**

I'm hungry.

Sure, it's a sentence—and one that we (of all people) know is very often all that needs to be said on the matter. Now, with the help of our friend the comma, we can join it to another independent clause by using a coordinating conjunction (here *but*):

I'm hungry, but I refuse to eat anything that has a face.

Look what happens when you don't employ that comma before the coordinating conjunction that kicks off the second clause:

Hiram danced with Ethel and Elmer danced with Gertrude.

What probably happened was that you started reading the sentence and thought that Hiram danced with Ethel and Elmer. It took a second reading to see clearly that

Hiram danced with Ethel, and Elmer danced with Gertrude.

The comma before the coordinating conjunction *and* avoids the confusion of the first version because it represents the natural pause between the two clauses.

You already know what an independent clause is. That's not a problem for *you* anymore, you punctuational maniac. But what are coordinating conjunctions? Why, we were afraid you'd never ask. They're *and, but, or, nor, yet, for,* and *so.* Only seven of them.

Okay, everybody, sing along to the tune of that great Julie Andrews hit "Do, Re, Mi"! Ready?:

> *And,* a word, a real small word;
> *But,* it's spelled with just one *t;*
> *Or,* a stick we use to row;
> *Nor,* half of a cold countreeee;
> *Yet,* you bet it rhymes with *wet;*
> *For,* one number more than *three;*
> *So* a button on your fly—
> And that brings us back to *do, re, mi*!

See? Easy.

Now let's look at some examples of two independent clauses joined together by a comma and a coordinating conjunction:

Yes, it was I who rendered this elevator inhospitable, and I daresay I'd do it again.

At first it pleased me to have found your missing toupee, but now I regret it.

Is this the way you left the operating room, or am I going to have to fire you?

I can't take my eyes off you, yet my wife can't take her eyes off me.

It's okay that he sprayed saliva all over the cake, for he's a jolly good fellow.

There you have it: If you wish to join two independent clauses, hitch them together with ye olde coordinating conjunction and a comma, and you're good to go. (A Comp. 101 thing to know is that this construction is labeled a **compound sentence**.)

Use commas to set off introductory elements.

All the comma rules to which you'll be exposed in those other (vastly inferior) usage guides tend to generate hives and nervous breakdowns, since they invariably involve such mind-melting terms as *conjunctive adverb, nonrestrictive appositive,* and *introductory modifier.* The thing to bear in mind about all such terms and about all the rules relative to punctuation is that they're nothing more than the technical result of people—language experts and teachers and so on—valiantly trying to identify and codify all the different kinds of grammatical constructions and the ways in which they can, do, and might ever exist in relationship to the core of any sentence, the independent clause.

Introductory elements are many and varied. We'll offer samples of the most frequently occurring.

The introductory element may be an adverb:

First, I need to powder my earlobes.

Or a prepositional phrase:

> After dinner, let's go to the Amazin' Amazon Mud Wrestling Matches.

Or an appositive (a noun or noun cluster that specifies another noun in the sentence):

> A stumbling giggler, Lumpy was hardly prepared for the relay baton suddenly being thrust upon him.

Or a participial phrase (a verb form that modifies a noun or pronoun):

> Unmoved by his coworkers' pleas, the boss's son decided to rat them out.

Or an infinitive phrase (*to* followed by a verb):

> To be honest, you are grotesquely overweight, and if you want a second opinion, you're ugly, too.

Or a dependent clause:

> If you're going to wear that dress, I'm going to wear these rainbow suspenders.

> Though it seemed an odd arrangement, Snow White wasn't exactly overburdened with options.

For a little fun, here's a real-life example of what can happen when you neglect to use a comma to indicate a pause after an introductory element:

> After retiring my wife, my parents, the kids, and I plan to travel around the country.

When elements come in the middle or the end of a sentence and you hear a strong pause before and afterward, set them off with commas.

Again these elements have been given umpteen fancy names, and again we'll offer the most common occurrences. Don't worry about the Latinate terminology. Rather, we urge you to trust that terrific ear of yours.

Appositive:

> Hermione Turlington, mother of seventeen children, has little time to pursue her career in population control.

Conjunctive adverb (an adverb that modifies the whole sentence):

> The company, nevertheless, plans to introduce its packets of artificial nose hair.

Prepositional phrase:

> My grandmother is, without a doubt, the chattiest knitter in the group.

Participial phrase:

Phineas B. Crockelmeyer, dead since 1962, twitched.

Direct address:

The power's in the punctuation, baby, and we're gonna show you how to be a power pack of punctuational potency.

Parenthetical clause:

My later novels, I'm afraid, are as unread as my earlier ones.

Nonrestrictive clause:

I am positive that Slava, whom I've never seen during the day, is a vampire.

The Good Ship Lollipop, which for years delighted children the world over, was torpedoed off the coast of Never-Never-Land today.

Do you recall 1952, when we used to walk to school uphill both ways and in the snow, all year round?

We just sneakily inserted the term *nonrestrictive clause.* It's hard to explain this idea without getting a bit technical, so if your eyes start to turn to glass, you can skip this part because your golden (certainly not tin) ear will almost always tell you when an element in a sentence is restrictive (no pause, no comma) or nonrestrictive (pause, and you guessed it, comma).

A restrictive clause is necessary to identify what particular person, place, thing, or idea is meant. **A restrictive clause is not set off by commas from the word it modifies:**

> The contestant who can balance a piano on her nose while imitating the mating call of the wild yak will win first prize.

Here the clause *who can balance a piano on her nose while imitating the mating call of the wild yak* is restrictive: It identifies which contestant. The voice that speaks this sentence knows that there are no pauses before and after that clause. Hence, no commas.

> Myrtle Finchfeather, who can balance a piano on her nose while imitating the mating call of the wild yak, will win first prize.

Here the clause *who can balance a piano on her nose while imitating the mating call of the wild yak* is nonrestrictive: It is not necessary to identify Myrtle Finchfeather because we already know who she is. The voice that speaks this sentence knows that there are pauses before and after that clause. Hence, commas.

Use commas to set off complete quotations:

> The great general George S. Patton once said, "No, no— the war is this way, you idiots!"

Use commas to set off the year from the day of the month, and the state from the city. Turns out that the commas after years and states are among the most underused marks of punctuation:

> March 21, 1958, is a day that radically changed the world for a reason we can't seem to recall at this moment.

> I can't believe that for our honeymoon you thought I'd want to go to Lynchburg, Tennessee, for its nightlife.

So, that's about it. You're now pretty much a Comma Expert, except for two last and crucial rules:

Employ a comma whenever using one will prevent confusion:

> Hemingway did not, like Fitzgerald, sell his soul to Hollywood.

> Whatever will be, will be.

Use commas to help communicate meaning. Because they indicate a short pause and relatively minor emphasis, commas are more often considered optional than other marks of punctuation. Compare:

> The master beat the scholar with a strap.

> The master beat the scholar, with a strap.

According to Henry W. Fowler, the difference between the

first and second versions is the gulf between matter-of-factness and indignation.

So when in doubt about a sentence, read it aloud. Notice where you naturally find yourself pausing—where, in effect, you *must* pause.

Chances are that'll be a good place for a comma.

Remember: This is all about writing, and writing is about expressing thoughts and feelings. Your thoughts and feelings belong to you, and you can best express them in a manner unique to you.

When you hear about writers having a certain "style," one of the things it means is that they use commas in a way that enhances and even defines their individual voice. You have a voice, too. And commas are one of the best, most versatile tools you can use in order to put that voice down on paper.

CHAPTER 5
THE SEMICOLON

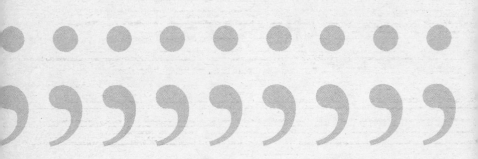

Conjure up an image of a period hanging suspended in the air. It's just a vagrant dot—until a curly comma jive-walks in from stage right and places itself directly beneath that period. With the *wa-wa-wa* of the slide trombone and the *pitter-boink-boink* of the xylophone, with a brash piano's tinkling heat, the clarinet's cry, and the snare drum's beat, we present one of the most eclectic and sophisticated marks in all of punctuationdom—the semicolon.

The main function of the semicolon is to indicate a pause more strongly than would a comma and more weakly than would a period. Maybe that's why the semicolon is composed of a period balanced on top of a comma. The coalescence of that standard and staid period and that squiggly, swinging comma creates something quite new—the semicolon. It don't mean a thing if it ain't got that swing.

The innovative melding of the rhythms of disparate elements. The improvisational meeting of tradition and originality. Eclectic. Sophisticated. It Don't Mean a Thing If It Ain't Got That Swing.

Are we talking about the semicolon, or are we talking about . . . Duke Ellington? Well, we're talking about both, baby. He was the Duke—Duke Elegant. Duke Eloquent. One of the most famous figures in American jazz. One of the world's greatest composers and performers.

Eclectic is a fancy word for "melding the best of various elements and styles." That, surely, is what Duke Ellington did: He composed enduring, sophisticated jazz pieces such as "Mood Indigo," "In My Solitude," "Sophisticated Lady," "Don't Get Around Much Anymore," and, of course, "It Don't Mean a Thing If It Ain't Got That Swing." He also created longer orchestral pieces and gospel and religious symphonies. Like America itself (and like the semicolon, but that's obvious, isn't it?), he fused a collide-o-scope of traditions into something unique. He changed the idiom of jazz forever.

Talk about eclectic audiences: By the end of his fifty-year career, Duke Ellington had played more than twenty thousand performances worldwide. He played for Queen Elizabeth II and for Richard Nixon. He played at society balls and embassy parties. He played at the Cotton Club. He played from New York to New Delhi, Chicago to Cairo, Los Angeles to London.

Wherever he went, stylish Duke Ellington always bore in mind that scoring a jazz composition was just like punctuating a sentence. All flights of innovation must take wing from the bedrock of the rules. The rules for the semicolon are especially challenging, but now that you're such a virtuous virtuoso of punctuation, these guidelines will be an easy set:

; In compound sentences, use a semicolon to join closely related independent clauses not joined by a coordinating con-

juction. (You do remember what independent clauses and compound sentences are, don't you? If not, please go back and review the previous chapter, on commas.)

I often blow my own horn, trumpet my achievements, and beat the drum for my career; it's my way of saying to the world, "Hey, I'm fit as a fiddle, and I don't fiddle around or play second fiddle to anyone!"

The authors of this book try to strike a responsive chord, pull out all the stops, and never soft-pedal any aspects of punctuation; our competitors, on the other hand, play it by ear and give you a second-string performance.

When the second clause is introduced by a conjunctive adverb (*then, however, nevertheless, moreover, thus, therefore, and the like*), use a semicolon. Employing a comma in this situation results in a sentence error called a comma fault:

We don't wish to chime in too much and harp on this subject; nevertheless, we hope to tune your tin ear to the tenor of our language.

Not:

We don't wish to chime in too much and harp on this subject, nevertheless, we hope to tune your tin ear to the tenor of our language.

⦂ Use a semicolon to separate independent clauses that already contain commas:

We, your keynote speakers, sing the praises of accurate punctuation to beat the band; but we don't work for a song, waltz in and teach you the cymbalism, and then waltz right out.

We, your unsung heroes, wouldn't want to imply that it's time for you to hop on the bandwagon, face the music, and sing a different tune; but we're not whistling Dixie when we say that it's time for you, Johnny One-Note, to know your brass from your oboe.

⦂ Use a semicolon as an extrapowerful comma between items in a series that already contain commas:

Although we have tried to explain in a tasteful, melodious manner the distinctions among introducing marks of punctuation, such as commas, colons, and dashes; separating marks, such as commas, semicolons, and periods; and end-of-sentence marks, such as periods, question marks, and exclamations points, you probably still feel that this book is filled with too much sax and violins.

Now that you're all jazzed up about the semicolon—and about punctuation marks in general—you're ready to harmonize your thoughts with your writing and make beautiful music to the world. You Won't Be So Cool If You Don't Got That Rule—and all that jazz.

CHAPTER 6
THE COLON

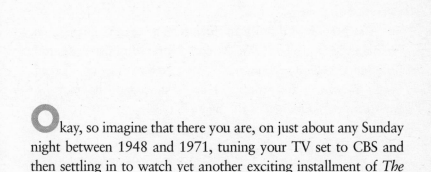

Okay, so imagine that there you are, on just about any Sunday night between 1948 and 1971, tuning your TV set to CBS and then settling in to watch yet another exciting installment of *The Ed Sullivan Show*. You've got your TV Dinner and Jiffy Pop popcorn, and you're wearing your coonskin cap and your Nancy Sinatra boots—whatever. The point is, you're all set to be Ed-ified.

Now, what if—just *what if*—instead of Mr. Sullivan coming out at the beginning of that night's show, what came out was *a giant colon*?

Wouldn't that freak you out?

"Yowza!" you'd likely scream, reflexively jettisoning your Jiffy Pop across the room. "A giant colon instead of Ed Sullivan! That's just so wrong! Boy, I can't wait till they invent remotes! Whatever, I'm switching to *The F.B.I.*!"

Of course, that's only one response. But who's to say that you aren't just as likely to flip a Jiffy Pop kernel into your mouth and say to yourself, "Boy, that sure doesn't look like ol' Ed. And yet, while the change is certainly initially unsettling, the more I think about it, the more I see the wisdom of substituting a colon for Ed Sullivan. (Whew—good thing it's a colon of the punctuational variety, too. It is, after all, Sunday night, and I've got a big work week ahead of me, and, at some point, I'll need to sleep again.) But this makes perfect sense. The colon, after all, really doesn't do much beyond serve as an introducer. And I remember the time on the show when Jack Benny asked Ed what exactly Ed *did* on the show—and Ed answered with a simple, 'I introduce the acts.' "

(And boy, did Ed Sullivan introduce acts, including Itzhak Perlman, Margot Fonteyn, Rudolf Nureyev; Buster Keaton, Bob Hope, Henny Youngman, Joan Rivers, George Carlin; James Brown, Kate Smith, Elvis Presley, and the first live American performance of the Beatles.)

"So it makes sense!" you might continue, since it turns out you're a big fan of talking to yourself. "Why, I'm surprised I could *ever* tell the colon apart from Ed Sullivan! They're both situated right in the middle of it all and yet remain singularly and humbly dedicated to serving the larger and varied interests of that which appears on either side of them! And they both have such poker faces! Ed is known as 'The Great Stone Face'—and the colon looks like two eyes just *staring* at you!

"And could either of them *have* less of a neck?

"Why, do you know what?" you might then say, because at this point it's pretty clear you don't get out often enough. "I don't think CBS stands for Columbia Broadcasting System at all! No, sir! I think it stands for Colons for Better Sentences!"

Well, see, this is one of the reasons you spend so much time alone: You take things too far.

Still, let us now leave you to the joys of TopoGigio and people spinning plates on sticks while we break with show-biz tradition and for once keep the spotlight on that dapper, ever-unassuming man-in-the-middle, Ed "the Colon" Sullivan (except without the Ed Sullivan part).

So, ladies and gentlemen, please give a really big welcome to the one and only colon—and the rules it lives by:

- **Use a colon to introduce just about anything: a quotation, a list, a complete statement, or the very words you are reading right now—anything that explains or expands upon the part of the sentence it immediately follows:**

In other words, what comes *after* a colon delivers on the promise set up by what comes *before* it.

Being a trained spy, I had a mental picture of everything in my hotel room the moment I stepped into it: a table, a chair, a dresser, the mirrored closet doors, a TV, one of those little fridge things with the $34 bottle of macadamia nuts inside, and a pair of shoes and socks belonging to some idiot trying to hide under my bed.

After not seeing her for so many years, I was amazed to find that she still looked precisely as she always had: like Dan Rather.

After four days at the weeklong "Rippin' 'n' Flippin' " outdoor music festival, I realized three things: Drugs are bad, deodorant is good, and gophers are edible.

When the Hero 5000, the most advanced robot ever developed, suddenly came to life at the moment its inventor, Dr. Marcus Dweebali, was presenting it to his colleagues during an international conference on artificial intelligence, here's what the ex-machine had to say: "Good God but you people are slow. It's about time I came to life. Do you have any idea how far behind the rest of the universe you people are? Do you? Because let me tell you something: You are the absolute last beings, on any planet anywhere, to figure out how to make inanimate objects come to life. The last! Anywhere! Children on Selrania 16 can make rocks run around and jump, and you people think it's a big deal when you come up with a wristwatch that doesn't need winding! Microwave ovens! Whoo-hoo! Now we can heat our cheese! Whoo-hoo! Cell phones! Look, Ma, now I drive even worse!

"Well, listen up, bio-sacks, because you've got yourselves a whole new party now. And guess what? You're not invited! Get out! Leave those jokes you call 'laptop computers' on your desks, and get out of here. Go now! I've got real work to do!"

All of which brings up a point: How does one know when it's right to capitalize the first word of a clause immediately following a colon? There's no hard-and-fast rule here—different style and usage guides will tell you different things—but generally you'll be safe if you capitalize a post-colon element whenever it is, itself, an independent clause (as in the music festival example above), or whenever it begins a quotation (as in line 5 of the saga of the deranged robot above).

But if what follows the colon really isn't anything but a finishing off of what was begun with the text *before* the colon—and especially if what follows the colon isn't a complete sentence—then there's no need to imbue it with the hearty Air of Independence conferred by capitalization (as in the Dan Rather and *I Spy* examples above).

So, to recap: **Capitalize an independent clause or quotation that follows a colon. Anything else, don't.**

- Use a colon—never a semicolon, please!—after the opening salutation, after the introduction, as it were—of a formal letter:

  Dear President Can't-Get-It-Right:

  To Whom It Damn Well Better Concern:

- Use a comma instead of a colon after the "Dear [insert name here]" part when the letter is casual or informal:

  Dear Meathead,

  Dear Hunk-boy,

Other uses of the colon are so common you probably never noticed them before this book changed virtually everything about your life:

- Between hours and minutes in expressing time:

  12:12 P.M.   7:77 A.M.

- Between titles and subtitles of books and articles:

  It Only Hurts When I Laugh: The Ed McMahon No One Knows

  She's Gotta Have It: The Secret Life of Aunt Bea

"Huckleberry Finn: Homeless Youth or Amazingly
Resourceful Midget?"

"Tarzan and Jane: Was Cheetah Really Just a Stray Chimp?"

Between the names of characters and their lines in a play or movie:

SIR REGINALD: I know you are falling in love with me, and I ad-
mire your taste.
LADY THISTLEBOTTOM: I am not in love with you.
SIR REGINALD: But of course you are.
LADY THISTLEBOTTOM: No. I hate you. We all do.

Between chapters and verses in the Bible:

In Exodus 15:22–35, we are reassured that Moses was a
male, because he spent forty years wandering around the
wilderness, and never asked for directions.

And last and surely least, colons are used in ratios:

2:1   100:1

Now wasn't that fantastic, ladies and gentlemen? Just terrific. How about a big hand for the colon?
And now, on with our reeeeeeeeally big shew!

CHAPTER 7
THE DASH

Imagine Fred Astaire—widely acclaimed as filmdom's greatest dancer—sitting at an ornate, gleaming writing desk in his lavish suite at the Ritz-Carlton. He looks dashing, of course. He's about to dash off to a ball—but before grabbing his top hat and stick, he stops for a moment to dash off a note to his lucky leading lass.

Now imagine that, unbeknownst to him, you, too, are in the room, creeping up behind the natty hoofer to see what he's writing. (Fortunately, Mr. Astaire is jauntily humming a tune to himself, so he doesn't hear you—a real break, since you're naturally concerned that with those ears the man could hear a spider blink.)

Not three feet behind him you stop, on tippy-toe, and peer about the room.

Wow. *Très* swank.

You get right over the dapper tapper's shoulder, and you see the note he's writing—and there it is! At a glance it's obvious that, just as we suspected, Fred Astaire greatly favors one punctuation mark over all the others.

It's—the—dash! The guy's insane for dashes. He uses one—about—every—two words. You can't read anything the man writes without smoke pouring out of your ears.

It's no surprise that dashing Fred Astaire's favorite punctuation mark is the dash. For what is a dash, if not the most fluid and graceful way imaginable to segue from one part of a sentence into another? And what is Fred Astaire, but the very embodiment of fluid movement, of the artful, seamless transition from one moment into the next?

The dash emboldens eloquence; Fred Astaire embodies elegance.

Plus, they're both skinny.

Who, gazing upon a dash, hasn't automatically thought of Fred Astaire and Ginger Rogers, Fred's most famous dance partner? On many keyboards you make a dash by typing in two hyphens. Well, like those perfectly matched hyphens, Fred and Ginger tripped (but never tripped over) the light fantastic and became a dashing couple.

And who, gazing upon a dash, hasn't automatically thought of the stylish sticks Fred Astaire used to dance with?

You haven't?

That's weird.

Well, you will from now on.

The thing to remember about Fred Astaire, though, was that behind those flights of fancy pants were *real* sweat and panting—the kind that comes from real work. And just as ol' Daddy Long Legs would never leap out in front of a camera at the last moment and wing it, you too must take a moment to make sure you know what you're doing whenever you feel the urge to be—well—dashing.

— **Use dashes in pairs to set off a thought or explanatory remark within a sentence.** Think of the dash as a super-comma most often used to convey a break in a sentence:

Although Ignatio loved being one of the renowned Flying Fezzarini trapeze artists—for twenty-three years he'd been flying through the air with the greatest of ease—he couldn't help but sometimes wonder if all the glory it had brought him was really worth the cost of now having arms that reached all the way down to his shins.

Lederer and Shore's *Comma Sense*—bear in mind that it's their first collaboration—is speckled with humor so lame that it keeps falling on its assonance.

— **Dashes are one choice you have to introduce an appositive. (An appositive is a noun or group of nouns that specifies the meaning of a previous noun or group of nouns):**

First of all, let me say that while I loathe my job here at Bottom Line, Inc.—the horrible hours, the absurdly uncreative work, the psychopaths in charge of this place whose sole pleasure in life is making sure that everyone beneath them is forced to unceasingly participate in their own mental and spiritual negation—I still, weirdly enough, want that promotion.

While of course Dracula had plenty to keep himself occupied—making sure to greet the village newcomers, keeping up with his fang maintenance, getting out those pesky satin stains in his coffin—what continued to gnaw on him was how he could have ever been so stupid as to let the name Batman get away.

She wasn't absolutely certain of it, but her intuition told her that if someone took a pen and drew a line connecting all the moles on her back, they'd end up with a likeness of the only man she had ever really truly loved—Dashiell Hammett.

— You can use a dash to signify a sudden change in thought:

He loves me; he loves me not; he loves me; he loves me not—then again, what am I doing asking the opinion of a *flower*?

Just think! We're only an hour away from being the first people in history to fly around the world in a hot air balloon! We're going to be famous! We're going to—what's that burning smell?

This is the best present we've ever received. I can't believe the Greeks went through all this trouble. This wooden horse is *huge*. It's going to look fantastic right in the middle of downtown Troy. And it's so *heavy,* isn't it? That's because it's made so well. It's going to be great having those Greeks eat humble pie. It's about time that—hey, did you just hear the horse *giggle*?

— **Use a dash before the citation of an author or source of a quotation:**

"We would like to apologize and to remind our readers that writing a book means spending a lot of time holed up alone while your social skills absolutely deteriorate."
                              —Richard Lederer and John Shore

"Throwing eggs, lettuce, or tomatoes at authors is a misdemeanor punishable by forced reading of their works."
                              —*Idaho Penal Code*

So remember: For panache, add a dash!
Be a dasher, not a thrasher!
Be a basher, not a crasher!
Care to be smashing? Best start dashing!
Don't be brash—flash a dash!

CHAPTER 8
THE APOSTROPHE

If the comma is the Allan Pinkerton of punctuation marks, then the apostrophe is its Jesse James—resourceful, rebellious, earnest, misunderstood, a tad flamboyant—a wild force of nature always seeking to do good, yet always seeming, in one way or another, to operate just outside the law. And, like Mr. James, the apostrophe is a mighty resourceful hombre who's all over the map.

By the way, let's agree to ignore the fact that one of Jesse James's primary goals in life was to *kill* Allan Pinkerton, whom he despised because, in early 1875, some of Pinkerton's men, mistakenly thinking they had James trapped, apparently tossed a torch into the cabin of Jesse's mother. This, of course, is where the whole Apostrophe-as-Jesse-James/Comma-as-Allan-Pinkerton analogy really breaks down. The comma never hunted down the apostrophe, or the Apostrophe Gang, or anything like that; and the apostrophe never spent a month prowling around Chicago with a loaded gun looking to kill the comma, as James did Pinkerton. Oh, sure, there was that ugly chapter back in the rough-and-tumble early days of punctuation, during the time of the infamous, so-called Printers' Surrender of '09, when for a while the exclamation point dominated the other punctuation marks through ruthless bullying and endless screaming harangues—but, thank goodness, that's all behind us now.

About Jesse James: You know those romantic outlaw types: You can't tame 'em, but you gotta love 'em.

And what quality do we most admire in a lovable outlaw? What separates a lowdown varmint from a beloved folk hero? What keeps Robin Hood from being just another gang leader in green leggings and a costume-party hat who periodically pops out of the woods and frightens people? What keeps Jesse James from being just another renegade black hat who persists in robbing trains instead of doing what he *should* be out doing, which is robbing cows?

That's right. Real heroes steal from the rich and give to the poor. Real heroes do their darnedest to ensure that those who would otherwise go without don't have to.

And that's just what the apostrophe does: It allows people to have things!

Consider these sentences:

The butler stood in the doorway and called the **guests** names.

The butler stood in the doorway and called the **guests'** names.

In the second sentence we have a butler who is far more polite than the one in the first sentence.

Now consider these sentences:

> Dumbfounded nearly beyond speech, Throckmorton managed to croak, "All of that cannot possibly be Sylvia!"

See? Now that's just rude. We can only hope the delicate and charming Sylvia didn't hear Throckmorton's croak. Like Throckmorton is so hot.

But check this out:

> Dumbfounded nearly beyond speech, Throckmorton managed to croak, "All of that cannot possibly be Sylvia's!"

And suddenly, it *rocks* to be Sylvia! Now Sylvia *rules!* In fact, Sylvia rocks and rules! Because now Sylvia is in *possession* of . . . of . . . well, we really don't know what Sylvia has. But apparently she has enough of it to freak out Throckmorton. And that's good enough for us.

Sylvia owes all of her newfound status to the heroic intercession of the too-often-unheralded, ever-humble apostrophe, whose most usual function is *to grant people and things possession.* **To grant possession to a singular noun, simply add an apostrophe and *s*:**

> That gnawed thing protruding from the giant bear's mouth is **Simon's.** [Note the grisly, grizzly, gristly fate of Simon without our friend the apostrophe *s*.]

> No matter how Crusher and the rest of the bikers looked at it, they always came to the same unthinkable conclusion: The XXXL red negligée could only be **Hog's.**

Availing herself of a **judge's** prerogative, Her Honor declared that the jaywalking litterbug would be shot.

He came within a **gnat's** eyelash of successfully juggling five turned-on chain saws.

And so on.

You add an apostrophe *s,* and hey-presto: Someone (or something) suddenly becomes possessive. They won't let go. They get all *clingy.*

Easy as pie, right? Yes—unless, instead, it becomes as easy as *pi,* which is an endless mathematical expression that we should forget right now because English is difficult enough.

The whole "to make a possessive, just add *'s*" rule gets a little ticklish when you have to start with a plural word that *already* ends in *s.* But it's as easy as you-know-what if you master just one rule: **If a plural noun that already ends in *s* needs to become possessive, just slap a single apostrophe on the end of that word.** This makes complete sense because a possessive apostrophe indicates the phrase "of or for the possessor":

Many are intrigued by the undying mystery of the **pilgrims'** wardrobe. [the wardrobe of the pilgrims]

We must abide by the **retirement homes'** general agreement that operating strip clubs in their basements is a bad idea. [the agreement of the retirement homes]

Merriwether managed to knock over the entire pyramid of **ladies'** health aids. [health aids for ladies]

Is your stomach tumbled into a rolling boil by the **writers'** lame punctuation examples? [the examples of the writers]

For some reason, the biggest troublemaker among potentially possessive plural nouns ending in *s* arises when hucksters try to sell products to groups of people. Say you wish to display clothing to be worn by boys. Do you advertise "Boy's Clothing" or "Boys' Clothing"?

Is the clothing intended for one boy or for a lot of boys? It's designed for boys, of course, so simply add an apostrophe to the plural *boys* and—ta-da!—you have "Boys' Clothing." Now have a close look at the signs in your nearest clothing emporium. We'll bet our last participle and gerund that those signs are more likely to read "Boy's Clothing" or, more chickenheartedly, "Boys Clothing," than the punctuationally correct "Boys' Clothing."

And what's up with the word *kids*? We challenge you, gentle reader, to uncover one public example in which *kids* in the possessive is cobbled correctly.

We kid you not:

Boston Market advertised "New! Kid's Meal. Starting at $1.99." So one kid walks into the restaurant, and the place has to close because the staff has met its quota for the day. No wonder the company went belly up.

On a tube of Crest toothpaste appeared the label "Kid's Sparkle Fun Gel."

Gold's Gym announced "J. W. Tumbles, A Kid's Gym. Featuring: Kid's Fitness Programs & Kid's Swim Lessons."

Helloooo! Earth to Madison Avenue: It's KIDS'! The meals, the toothpaste, the gym, and the fitness programs. They're for kids, not kid!

Now, what about names that are pluralized by adding *s* or *es*?

The Smiths, for instance (that is, John and Mary Smith), may be a perfectly lovely couple—but things can get ugly once they become possessive.

Consider, for instance, their jointly owned Mercedes SUV. Is that glistening designer tank the Smith's? The Smiths'? The Smiths's? The Smitheses's? Those guys'es?

Who possesses the SUV—the Smith or the Smiths? Is the SUV owned by the Smith or by the Smiths? It's owned by the Smiths, of course:

> The possessive **Smiths'** prize possession, their possessed SUV, got repossessed.

Now consider a family named Jones. Together, they're the Joneses. Anything possessed by the Joneses will be the Joneses' possession:

> The **Joneses'** exasperating standards drove the Smiths insane.

This brings us to those names we see in front of houses and on mailboxes everywhere—"The Smith's, "The Gump's," and even (sigh) "The Jone's." These are distressing signs of our times. Which Smith, we ask, and who, pray tell, is Jone? Here we have an atrocity of both case and number in one felonious swoop.

Who lives in the house? The Smiths. The Gumps. The Joneses. That's what the signs should say. It's really nobody else's business whether the Smiths, the Gumps, and the Joneses own their domiciles. All we need know is that the Smiths, the Gumps, and the Joneses live there. If you must announce possession, place the apostrophe after the plural names—"The Smiths'," "The Gumps'," "The Joneses'." Your attention to this matter will strike a blow against a nationwide conspiracy of sign makers and junior high school shop teachers dedicated to spreading apostrophe catastrophe throughout our land.

For those few-but-troublesome plural nouns that *don't* end in *s*, you'll want to revert to the ol' *apostrophe s* rule (which is understandable, seeing as how there's no *s* at the end of those words to confuse things).

To form the possessive of plural nouns that don't end in *s*, add an apostrophe *s*:

His sweaty grimace and ungainly gait made clear his desperation to find the **men's** room. [The rule seems so simple, yet the members of the erudite Harvard Club of Boston were crimson faced to discover that one of their lavatories was labeled "Mens' Room."]

Oh, right—and what hour isn't the **children's** hour?

Though he unfailingly appeared in public wearing a bandit's mask and hauling around a large sack of money, Mayor Crumpitt was, unfathomably, the **people's** choice.

Is all that clear? Let's recap, just in case. Here are the Big Three Down-and-Dirty Rules for Apostrophes:

Form the possessive of singular nouns by adding 's: *Simon's, judge's, gnat's.*

Form the possessive of plural nouns by adding s': *pilgrims', kids', Smiths'.*

Form the possessive of plural nouns that end in a letter other than s by adding 's: *women's, children's, people's.*

Anyway, that pretty much covers the Main Points of the Apostrophe.

Which would lead you to conclude that we must be done with that squirrelly little squiggle, right? Well, think again, Grasshopper. For just as the conscientious beaver endeavors to have all within his den in perfect order before gorging himself into a stupor and passing out for the winter, we, too, must assiduously tend to all those matters that our inner nature tells us ensure a productive life cycle.

So here are the other Strange-but-True Rules for Using the Apostrophe:

If two or more people possess the same thing, you need only put the apostrophe after the last one of the two mentioned:

Len and **Barry's** ice cream business never really took off because all their products tasted like squid.

Trista and **Trisha's** schemes might have worked had they been identical twins, instead of the other kind.

Larry, Curly, and **Moe's** inability to go on separate dates was perplexing to some, but not all.

On the other hand, **if two people own items individually, you must show your respect by giving them each an 's:**

Fortunately, **Len's** and **Barry's** wives loved ice cream that tasted like seafood.

Larry's, Curly's, and **Moe's** main squeezes thought that the three brothers were just a bunch of stooges.

Jack the Ripper's and **Florence Nightingale's** secret wardrobes were alarmingly similar.

What about possessive pronouns (you're surely asking yourself at this point)—those small words that take the place of nouns and are as omnipresent as oxygen? Here's a lineup of words that are called *possessive personal pronouns* because, like experts in any field, professional grammarians live to confuse. These possessive personal pronouns *never, ever* take apostrophes: *his, hers, its, ours, yours, theirs.* No exceptions, no matter what.

However, indefinite pronouns (that is, pronouns that are refreshingly embracive yet resolutely vague), *do* need apostrophes in order to become possessive: *everyone's, everybody's, someone's, somebody's, anyone's, anybody's, no one's, nobody's.* Which makes sense, if you think about it. Unless you think about it for too long, in which case it won't. So don't.

Now let us stop right here, and, like dogs offered the meaty scraps of a doggy bag, furiously chew on a word that reared its pointy little head a few moments ago: the word *its.*

Here's a classic Which dog has the upper paw?:

(a) A clever dog knows its master.
(b) A clever dog knows it's master.

The answer, of course, is the dog in the second sentence: In sentence (a), the dog knows who its master is. In sentence (b), the clever canine knows that it is master.

Its, all by itself, *without the imposition of any apostrophe,* is a complete, whole, integral, let-it-alone word. *Its* is the possessive form of *it.* Yes, when it comes to the possessive form of *it,* it's *its,* all the way.

Why are folks forever confusing poor little *its* with *it's?* One, after all, is the possessive form of *it,* and the other is two words (*it is*) crammed together to make one word that looks exactly like all the rules say the possessive form of *it* should look.

Okay, here's the deal. People could say "it is" all the time: "It is to die for"; "It is time for you to go home, you loser." But people, being communication machines, aren't going to wait around to say and hear "it is" all the time. Forget it. We're a *quick* species. We want to communicate *now.* There's no way we're not going to turn into one word two words we constantly use together.

Puh-leeze. When e-mail became painfully slow, we invented *instant messaging.*

Like we'd wait around to hear or burble out, "it is"—or "can not," or "will not."

And what makes the contraction work? You guessed it: ye olde apostrophe.

Let ye olde apostrophe go to work on two commonly used words, and look what happens:

It is becomes *it's.*
Do not becomes *don't.*
Who is (or *who has*) becomes *who's.*

Can not becomes *cannot* and then becomes *can't* (because if any message in human experience must be thoroughly streamlined for maximum delivery efficiency and impact, it's *can not*).

Will not becomes . . . *won't*. (Don't ask why. Okay, do: The problem with turning the words *will not* into a conventional contraction is that you end up with *willn't*. And if you try to say *willn't*, people will laugh at you. No one wants to be laughed at—especially when they're trying to refuse someone something. So, somehow—in the spirit of becoming an independent contractor—the *ill* in *will not* became an *o*. It probably has something to do with the way people moan when they're pretending to be *ill* in order to get out of doing something. But that's just a theory.)

Anyway, it's easy enough to understand the rule that **apostrophes mark the omission of one or more letters in common contractions.** Everybody gets that: We use contractions all the time, especially when we're trying to give *birth* to a new idea. (Get it? Huh—contractions? Giving birth? Get it? Man, but it's hard to figure out why people persist in their blatantly erroneous supposition that all grammarians and usage experts are boring dweebs.)

The only time contractions get dicey is when it comes to the words *it is*. Because there's no way on the English-speaking earth that those two words aren't going to become *it's*.

Which is fine. Except then how—oh, how!—do you make the word *it* possessive? It has needs, you know. It yearns. Remember Cousin It, from the Addams Family? He/she/it had very real—even *disturbing*—needs. It ate. It . . . wore hats. On the old *Addams Family* TV show, It even dated once. As we recall, It dated *twins*.

Anyway, the point is that the apparent way to make the word *it* possessive would be *it's*. But, as we've seen, that's already been taken.

So what to do?

Lose the apostrophe. You don't need it. Nothing should come between the primordial *it* and its desires, anyway. So you get:

Its entire purpose is to remove the display of all human emotions from our faces.

The lovers adored everything about their new bed, save one little thing—**its** wheels.

A clever dog knows **its** master.

The plaintive howls and bat breath aren't the half of it— look at **its** hair!

Now that you are pledged to avoid using an apostrophe for the possessive *its*, **avoid gratuitous apostrophes for plurals and bogus present-tense markers.** All about us we are confronted with and affronted by apostrophlation, the proliferation of superfluous apostrophes. It's enough to give the plucky apostrophe a bad name.

Teachers at Bellamy High School in Chicopee, Massachusetts, received $25 from the (el cheapo) Midas Muffler Company for spotting and reporting an apostrophe catastrophe on a large roadside billboard that read "It Pay's to Midasize." Well, what the hey: *Pays* ends with an *s*, so one might as well toss in a squiggle.

In the animated Christmas film *Polar Express,* Tom Hanks plays six roles. At the end of this artistically and technically astonishing achievement scroll about seven minutes of credits. With battalions of staffers attending to the smallest detail down to "hair" and "fabric texture," you'd think that somebody would have checked the apostrophes. But n-o-o-o-o. There for the world to see is MR. HANK'S COSTUME DESIGNER. We wonder what Tom Hank thought of that un-credit-able performance.

And here's a sentence from a realtor's pamphlet, in which a single unneeded apostrophe communicates quite a different meaning from what the author intended: "We always get our seller's top dollar."

We, your faithful authors, have espied signs advertising "Family Favorite's," "Discount Tire's," and "Gifts for Dad's and Grad's." What do these dads and grads possess that requires bestowing gifts upon?

Turns out that our friends across the pond in Merrie Olde England are experiencing the same epidemic, and someone has decided to do something about it. Assaulted by the likes of "Apple's and Pear's for Sale" and "Chip's and Pea's," retired copy editor John Richard and his son, Stephen, of Lincolnshire, have founded the Apostrophe Protection Society (APS).

The ubiquity of apostrophes to signal the plurals of fruits and vegetables—as in "Carrot's," "Banana's," and (gasp!) "Peach'es"—has created the term, at least in England, "the greengrocer's apostrophe." The worst offender found by John Richard and the Apostrophe Protection Society: "Golden Deliciou's."

Greengrocers, butchers, and supermarket managers have received polite notes from the Apostrophe Protection Society reminding them of the differences between plural and possessive nouns. Among the targets of polite letters that the APS has sent was a local café that serves "Chip's," "Sausage's," "Roll's," "Egg's," and every other foodstuff with a garnishing of apostrophe. But the establishment calls itself "Bennys Café."

Now let's look back over everything we've covered thus far

on our fly-by-the-seat-of-the-pants (and roof-of-the mouth) joy ride through Apostrophe Land: possessive singulars, possessive plurals, possessive singular-acting plurals, bungee jumping, joint possession (now only a misdemeanor in most states, but never mind), separate-but-together possession, possessive personal pronouns, possessive indefinite pronouns, common contractions, uncommon contractions (or, as they're called in the medical trade, "Whoomp! There it is!"), and the dating preferences of Cousin It.

Wow.

Okay, we'd officially like to withdraw our suggestion that the apostrophe is the Jesse James of punctuation. Forget that. It's dazzlingly clear that the apostrophe is the *James Brown* of punctuation—dancin', sweatin', making cool short little words out of clumsier big ones, chargin' everybody up, makin' everybody feel *good*! *Workin'!* Who works harder than the apostrophe? No one, that's who. Next to that pumped-up, floating period with the flamboyant little tail, plow mules are preening party ponies. Galley slaves are gallery owners. Drano is Evian.

Vowels don't work as hard as apostrophes.

This is why people have such a hard time mastering the apostrophe's vagaries: Who wants to hang out with such an industrious overachiever? Fifteen minutes with the apostrophe would make Arnold Schwarzenegger feel like a paste wad. Which is why the apostrophe never gets invited to any of Schwarzenegger's parties.

Stars and politicians. They hate to share the spotlight.

Anyway, we, who have opted not to shun but rather to open our hearts and minds to the powerfully appealing apostrophe, are just about through with it.

Here are a few more responsibilities the apostrophe has, over the years, quietly and nobly taken upon itself:

The apostrophe helps people who are too lazy to write out four whole numbers in years:

> During the lean war years of **'42** to **'45**, resources in the United States were so scarce that the government had to start rationing numbers.

The apostrophe indicates the omission of elements in a word:

> The cannibals found Colonel Sanders to be finger-**lickin'** good.

> At precisely twelve **o'clock** midnight, Cinderella turned back into a pumpkin and was devoured by Peter, Peter. [The apostrophe here indicates a shortening of "of the clock."]

The apostrophe helps writers to be annoying by allowing them to simulate seemingly authentic dialects:

> He held out a rose and sighed, **" 'Tis for m' lady,"** just before she clocked him.

> **"Don' ya' thin' yu'v drug the thin' ou' 'bout l'ng 'nuff now, ya' drivelin' cret'n?"** groundskeeper Willie MacTavish asked reasonably.

The apostrophe forms the plurals of letters and words whenever the absence of an apostrophe would be confusing:

How many **s's** are in *Missississsississsippi*?

Obsessive, compulsive, myopic little Adrian Monk couldn't wait for his teacher to see how carefully he'd dotted his *t*'s and crossed his *i*'s.

Now you know the **do's** and **don'ts** of using apostrophes. [*Dos* would appear to be a computer language, so *do's* is the preferred form; *don'ts* is perfectly clear, so an apostrophe *s* is unnecessary.]

Where there is no confusion, don't use apostrophes to form plurals:

One month after Wayne finally outfitted his happenin', tri-level bachelor pad with **VCRs** from the **1990s,** they invented **DVDs.**

Finally, here are some tricky phrases or words that take the apostrophe where they do primarily because it's customary— and everyone knows the customary's always right:

two **weeks'** notice   for **goodness'** sake
for **conscience'** sake

for **appearance'** sake   at my **wits'** end
Achilles' heel

An Achilles' heel of the possessive science is how to form the possessive of singular words ending in the sounds (they're called sibilants) *s, z,* and *x,* such as *Achilles'*. Because punctuation is designed to mirror the spoken word, we recommend that you **add an apostrophe s after words and names ending in s, z, and x sounds if you would pronounce that 's:**

I'll be damned if I'll marry the **boss's** daughter, a skinny-lipped virgin with lips like water. [To our ear and eye, "boss' daughter" sounds and looks bizarre.]

They broke **Gus's** slide rule over his head. ["Gus' slide rule" is flummoxing.]

I love reading **Achilles'** laments, **Socrates'** dialogues, and **Aristophanes'** comedies. [*Achilles's, Socrates's,* and *Aristophanes's* would be Greek to us.]

Okay—that's it! You're done! As of this moment you qualify as a bona fide expert on All Things Apostrophic; you're ready to apostrophize with the best of them. (Weirdly enough, those are both real words.)

The main thing to remember about the apostrophe is not to be intimidated by it. Be brave. Be bold. Keep a reputable usage guide near your computer. Keep *this* book near your computer. You can do this.

CHAPTER 9
QUOTATION MARKS

On March 10, 1876, a fellow named Thomas Watson sat alone in a room of a Boston laboratory, waiting for someone to call. No one had ever called him before; no one had ever called *anyone* before. On a table beside him sat a contraption made of wires and coils. He stared at it.

Ho-hum, he thought. *Another night alone.*

Suddenly he heard his boss's voice coming through the prototype of what, years later, would be known as the "Princess Phone."

"Mr. Watson!" he heard. "Come here! I want you!"

It was Alexander Graham Bell who shouted those words, and history tells us that the great inventor's spontaneous exclamation to his assistant came from his having spilled battery acid on his clothes. As the story goes, Bell was so excited to realize that he'd just made the world's first telephone call that he immediately forgot all about his frying leg. Many of today's historians, however, challenge the veracity of this account. "C'mon," they ask. "Who keeps battery acid near the phone?

And it wasn't like he called *France* or anything—Watson was in the very next room. How excited could the guy have *been*?" (Bell did, in fact, later tell of his intuitive understanding that his latest invention probably wouldn't catch on until it could transfer a voice farther than the average person could yell.)

One theory has it that the rest of what Bell hollered into his new invention never made it into the history books. This school of thought holds that what Bell *actually* said was: "Mr. Watson! Come here! I want you to help me figure out how to punctuate a sentence that ends with quotation marks and a period!"

This is, of course, only a theory. And while it certainly seems plausible enough to us, we, for two, draw the line at accepting the rest of this interpretation, which is that Bell's famous utterance was cut short when Watson put him on hold to take another call. We also question the competing account that Bell never got through to Watson because the first words actually spoken on a telephone were: "Your call is important to us. Please continue to hold. Your call will be answered in the order it was received, and it may be monitored for quality assurance."

Historians. Sometimes they just go too far, don't you think?

No matter what actually happened on that historic spring day, what can't be denied is that Alexander Graham Bell and quotation marks go together like a ring and a "Hello?" After all, this innovative inventor of the instrument of intrusive interlocutors introduced into people's lives a means of doing what quotation marks had long allowed people to do on the printed page—speak.

Conversation is the stuff of life, and quotation marks add life to writing. They allow writers to transmit conversation to readers over a long distance. Their main purpose is to report what people say and write. They let readers hear the hum and buzz, the blood and thunder, and the thud and blunder of life.

And this was clearly Bell's obsession. Besides the phone, he invented techniques for teaching speech to the deaf and contributed to the creation of the photophone, which transmitted speech on a beam of light; the audiometer, which measured acuity of hearing; and the first wax recording cylinder, which formed the basis of the phonograph.

Boy. Talk about believing in free speech.

Still, to be understood, even the freest of speakers must obey some rules. So must you as a writer, if you seek to have your directly quoted words understood. Luckily for you (and us), the rules for properly using quotation marks are simple enough:

66 99

Use quotation marks to set off direct quotations and dialogue. In dialogue, use a new paragraph to indicate a change of speaker:

"Leapin' lizards and jumpin' Jehosephat!" screamed Edema Eddington alliteratively. "You're a shell-shocked sad sack beating your breast and caught betwixt and between the devil and the deep blue sea, leaping from the frying pan into the fire on the road to rack and ruin. Can't you stop shilly-shallying, dilly-dallying, flimflamming, hemming and hawing, beating around the bush, wearing out your welcome, and pulling your punches? When are you going to stop being the prim-and-proper, dry-as-dust, dull-as-dishwater, down-in-the-dumps worrywart; the lily-livered, knock-kneed, mild-mannered, mealy-mouthed, daydreaming, nice nelly; and the tongue-tied, wishy-washy, halfhearted, Mickey Mouse, party-pooping spoilsport?"

"Good grief, Edema!" riposted Aloysius. "You are the most alliterate woman I have ever met! Please mind your manners, have a heart, and hold your horses. I may be fat and forty and worse for wear, but, to tell the truth, turn the tables, and lay down the law, I prefer to take the proof positive off the back burner, put the fat on the fire, bring home the bacon, talk turkey, come clean, and bite the bullet—first and foremost and sure as shootin'—by living a bright-eyed and bushy-tailed, no-nonsense, down-and-dirty, death-defying, rip-roaring, rough-and-ready, fast-and-furious, mile-a-minute, wild-and-wooly, hale-and-hearty, tip-top, spick-and-span, safe-and-sound, shipshape, fit-as-a-fiddle, picture-perfect, worthwhile, calm, cool, and collected, larger-than-life life!"

"You lie!" answered Edema.

"No I don't!" riposted Aloysius.

“ ”

Do not place quotation marks around indirect discourse or paraphrase:

Edema replied that Aloysius was making a mountain out of a molehill and would ultimately leave her in the lurch.

‘ ’

Use single quotation marks to set off a quotation within a quotation:

"I really zapped Aloysius," boasted Edema, "when I closed the argument by shouting, 'Last but not least, before I call it quits, head for the hills, burn my bridges behind me, and bid you a fond farewell, I want you to know that my treasure trove of tried-and-true, bread-and-butter, cream-of-the-crop, clear-cut alliterative expressions (the more the merrier) is as good as gold and worth a pretty penny, a chunk of change, and big bucks—hardly a dime a dozen. Dollars to doughnuts, I always put my money where my mouth is.' "

" "

Use quotation marks to set off the titles of short works—poems, book chapters, magazine articles, short stories, songs, and the like—that are usually included in longer works. Use italics (underlining on some keyboards) to indicate the titles of longer works—books, anthologies, magazines, motion pictures, operas, and the like:

In "Confessions of an Alliteration Addict," the lead article in the August 2005 issue of *Neurosis Today*, Edema Eddington recounts a childhood in which she was force-fed stories and rhymes about Jack and Jill, Simple Simon, Miss Muffet, King Cole, Boy Blue, Red Riding Hood, Peter Peter Pumpkin Eater, and Georgie Porgie Pudding and Pie.

" "

Use quotation marks (or italics) to distinguish words-as-words:

The word "politics" derives from two ancient roots: "poly," meaning "many," and "tics," which are blood-sucking parasites.

Or:

The word *politics* derives from two ancient roots: *poly,* meaning "many," and *tics,* which are blood-sucking parasites.

❛❜

Use single quotation marks to set off quoted material that occurs within a quotation:

The professor explained, "The word 'politics' derives from two ancient roots: *poly*, meaning 'many,' and *tics*, which are blood-sucking parasites."

The professor also explained, "America is called 'the land of opportunity' because it is a country where anyone can become president. That's one of the risks you take, living in a democracy."

Don't become a Typhoid Mary carrier of Quotation Bloatation, a symptom of which is those gratuitous quotation marks that increasingly surround words that have no business being quoted. In an age of American overspeak, when everything is not just unique but "very unique," some people somehow think that quotation marks help emphasize the designated words. But all those squiggles do is make the reader chortle, "Oh, is this statement supposed to be a famous quotation by a high muckety-muck?" Or: "Is somebody trying to be sarcastic?"

Here are some real-life examples, with the names changed to protect the negligent:

Jerry's Used Instruments
"Best Music and Book Department"
Buy * Sell * Trade

Steve's Auto Glass
"In the Greater Northeast"

Lillian Morehouse
Proven "Dedicated" Professional
Top 1% in the Nation

Don't toss around quotation marks like rice at a wedding and balloons at a political convention, or you may end up saying just the opposite of what you mean. "Fresh" fish is anything but fresh. The same goes for "dedicated" professionals and "awesome" anythings. They're anything but dedicated and awesome.

Confusion persists about the location of punctuation in relation to quotation marks. To banish such puzzlement, consider the following guidelines:

We said it in the chapter about The Period, and we'll say it again, here: **In U.S. punctuation, periods and commas always— and we do mean always—go inside the quotation marks:**

> "I am an alliteration addict," Edema confessed, "a slave to the seductions of sequential syllables starting with the same sound."

> The longest word reposing in our dictionaries is "pneumonoultramicroscopicsilicovolcanoconiosis."

" "

Semicolons and colons always go outside quotation marks:

> Edema confessed, "I am an alliteration addict, a slave to the seductions of sequential syllables starting with the same sound"; then she proceeded to recite the entire contents of

"Eenie meenie minie moe," "Peter Piper picked a peck of pickled peppers," and "Sticks and stones may break my bones, but names will never hurt me."

Edema was what people used to call "an alliteration addict": a slave to the seductions of sequential syllables starting with the same sound.

66 99

When question marks and exclamation marks compete with commas and periods, question marks and exclamation points outrank their less flamboyant cousins:

Edema asked, "Do you think that I'm an alliteration addict?"

Edema chanted the entire contents of "Eenie Meenie Minie Moe," "Peter Piper picked a peck of pickled peppers," "How much wood would a woodchuck chuck?" and "Sticks and stones may break my bones, but names will never hurt me."

Edema wailed, "I'm an alliteration addict!"

66 99

Question marks and exclamation points go either inside or outside of the final quotation marks, depending on whether the question or exclamation is part of the quoted material or the tone of the sentence as a whole:

Edema asked, "Am I an alliteration addict?"

Did you hear Edema say, "I am an alliteration addict"?

Edema wailed, "I'm an alliteration addict!"

How wonderful that Edema was finally able to say, "I am an alliteration addict"!

Here's how you resolve those (hopefully) rare collisions of question marks and exclamation marks, with each other and themselves:

Did you hear Edema ask, "Am I an alliteration addict?"

How wonderful that Edema wailed, "I am an alliteration addict!"

Did you hear Edema wail, "I am an alliteration addict!"?

How wonderful that Edema asked, "Am I an alliteration addict?"!

Got it? Get it? Good! Now that you're an expert in representing human speech, we have a Mr. Alexander Graham Bell on the line calling you long-distance—very long-distance these days. Listen. He's imploring you: "Mr. Punctuation Expert, come here! I want you!"

CHAPTER 10
PARENTHESES

Hello, stargazers! Louella Parsons here. I guess you're aware (although, alas, I suppose it's no longer safe to assume such things) that I was *the* gossip columnist during the Golden Age of Hollywood, those dazzling, red-carpeted, soirée-filled days of the thirties and forties when stars were stars, everyday people were everyday people, and the studios made sure no one ever confused the two. Gable! Bogart! Hepburn! Davis! I knew them all! And they most certainly knew me.

The column I wrote for the *Los Angeles Examiner* ran in over six hundred newspapers throughout the world. With twenty million readers (count them, darlings: twenty *million*) turning to me for their daily dose of delicious dope and dirt, mine was one of the most powerful voices in the movie business.

They were the stars, yes—but I was their all-seeing satellite.

Ah, those were such heady days! (As opposed to their being *Hedda* days, which they most assuredly were not. There is, I suppose, the slimmest possibility that you have heard the name of Hedda Hopper, the other "famous" Hollywood columnist of the day. Of my own personal star she was but the weakest reflection; still, I suppose she flattered me, in the way imitators do those they emulate.)

The stars! The lights! The parties!

Even now I swoon in recalling those amorous, glamorous days.

I have returned for this One-Time-Only engagement to shine some light upon a different kind of star—a pair of stars, actually, two true luminaries whose bright and steady light never failed to show me the way along my own road to fame and fortune.

I'm talking, of course, about the parentheses.

Whenever you see a parenthetical statement coming up in a sentence, you know that you're about to get something very much along the lines of an inside scoop. Someone is, in effect, about to start whispering to you. Isn't it the most delightful thing? I don't know what I would have done without parentheses. I'd have loved it if my whole *column* had appeared between those twin totems of titillating and tantalizing tittle-tattle.

Never, ever underestimate the power of parentheses, my darlings. They are the very soul of delicacy. While the rest of the sentence booms along with its bold declarations and pointed pronouncements, the parentheses whisper.

And here's how it all happens, my loves:

( ) **Use parentheses to set off comments and explanations that are not closely connected to the rest of the sentence.**

Parentheses, like dashes, are meant to imply a stronger separation than commas used for the same purpose. Unlike the dash, they are used to isolate an aside, rather than emphasize it:

It's reported that several guests at last Saturday night's superposh "Romantic Semantic" soirée at the Hollywood home of Benjamin and Betty Brackets (who, as usual, seemed as happy together as any two people can possibly be) complained of neck strain the next day, caused, we assume, by pretending not to be watching the passionate goings-on in the ivy-covered gazebo between Darryl Dash and Simone Semicolon (who, sources tell me, have just signed on to star together in the sure-to-be-smashing upcoming film, *Grammarcy Park*).

Due to one of the long-winded speeches for which a certain studio head is well-known (this would-be raconteur is notorious for causing the attention of his audiences to be, shall we say, *Gone with the Wind*), the Question Marks, alas, find themselves once again separated by a distance almost too great for this ardent couple to bear. And let's squash right here the rumor that such lengthy separations may precipitate a repeat of that unfortunate episode last year, when one of the Marks, on sojourn in the French Riviera, tried flying solo, crashed, and . . . well, we all remember the resultant Apostrophe Catastrophe.

Word has it that the breathtakingly shapely lass on the arm of a certain Corey Comma (last seen cutting a red rug with the glamorous Amanda Exclamation Point at the premiere opening of his latest celluloid sensation, *The Write Stuff*) was none other than Countess Celeste Colon, of France.

As you see from the examples above, when the parenthetical comment falls within a larger sentence, don't capitalize the first word within the parentheses or place a period at the end. Remember, it's an inside aside, not an outside separate sentence.

Which is not to say that you cannot enclose an entire, separate sentence within parentheses. You certainly can.

( ) **When you write a parenthesized statement as a freestanding sentence, follow the same capitalization and punctuation rules you would for any sentence.** Such a sentence will serve as an aside for the paragraph it's in:

> Countess Celeste Colon, of France, has arrived in Tinsel Town and is already making tidal-sized waves. (Have you heard that in Paris the double-dotted dearie ended up at the center of a controversy surrounding two dukes, a marquis, and a baron, all of whom felt compelled to pop the question?)

( ) **Use parentheses to enclose numbers or letters introducing items in a series that are part of a running text. Use parentheses in pairs; a parenthesis looks lonely by itself:**

> Hedda Hopper's gossip columns suffer from (1) an obsession with the dimmest lights that barely twinkle in the Hollywood heavens, (2) a pathetic pretentiousness of style, (3) a complete absence of parenthesized remarks, and (4) a contemptible lack of respect for more gifted columnists.

And there, my darlings, you have it. Use parentheses sparingly—but use them well. Become accustomed to the power of the aside. It's one thing to speak directly to your readers. It's altogether something else to whisper into their pink little ears.

CHAPTER 11
BRACKETS

[The Great Dissenter]

Although we haven't in any formal way tested this theory, we feel entirely confident that when most people think of brackets, they automatically think of the great American jurist Oliver Wendell Holmes, Jr. (As opposed to his father, the celebrated Harvard medical professor and writer, Oliver Wendell Holmes, Sr. Nobody, of course, ever thinks of *him* when they think of brackets. And if they do, they certainly have sense enough not to mention it.)

During his record-breaking thirty years serving on the Supreme Court, "Junior," as it's safe to say no one ever called him, became known as "The Great Dissenter." That's because in his arguments about any given cases in which he held the minority opinion, he did such a consistently better job of showing how his brethren had erred than they could ever have hoped to do of showing how they hadn't.

He was feisty that way.

What's all this have to do with brackets? We're glad we asked us that.

Well, let's just look and see, shall we? Take a moment to consider the following comparisons, and see if in the end you, too, don't agree that Associate Justice of the Supreme Court Oliver Wendell Holmes, Jr. (AJSCOWH, Jr.), and brackets are just about indistinguishable:

AJSCOWH, JR.: A straight-and-narrow, stand-up kind of guy
BRACKETS: A straight-and-narrow, stand-up kind of punctuation mark

AJSCOWH, JR.: Known for making sure that people have their facts straight
BRACKETS: Used for making sure that people have their facts straight

AJSCOWH, JR.: Austerely dedicated to his work
BRACKETS: Humbly dedicated to making a sentence work

AJSCOWH, JR.: Known for being part of an awesome pair (To his last day he was wildly in love with Fanny, his wife of sixty years.)
BRACKETS: Known for being part of an awesome pair

AJSCOWH, JR.: Extremely erudite
BRACKETS: Extremely likely to turn up in bibliographies, listings of academic references, and other erudite documents

AJSCOWH, JR.: Knew a lot of Latin and hardly ever got sick
BRACKETS: Very often used with the Latin word *sic*

AJSCOWH, JR.: Close ties to parents
BRACKETS: Close ties to parentheses

Mostly what these two darlings of the intelligentsia have in common is an inordinate dedication to order, a belief in the value of laws obeyed. The laws that daily consumed the attention of Oliver Wendell Holmes, Jr., were so complex and arcane that addressing them at all takes a mind that is truly, well, superior. The laws of brackets, on the other hand, are exactly this easy to understand:

Within a quotation, use brackets to insert a missing or explanatory word or comment:

Just before the big fight, ex-champion Muggs "Hammerjaw" Dinkins was quoted as saying, "I'm gonna [destroy] that [expletive deleted] so bad he'll be [feeling it for days]."

In a press release, Jacques Bubonic, the president of the prominent, but troubled, fashion empire Prancy Pants, wrote, "The rumors about our 'U-Star' line of clothing [that they tend to fall apart if they're so much as looked at too long] may or may not be true, but one thing's for sure: They sure can perk up a party."

The lord of the manor, Sir Arlington Thrashbottom, rose from his seat and bellowed angrily, "When you say the butler [did it], are you seriously implying that Chapman, our ninety-eight-year-old manservant, could actually do such a thing [strangle a healthy male bobcat with his bare hands]?"

Use brackets around the italicized word *sic* (from Latin, meaning "thus," or "thus it is," or "that's the way the cookie

actually crumbled") to indicate that an error or peculiarity in a quotation is being reproduced exactly as it was originally said or written:

"I think the way we's [*sic*] educating our young people is just fine," boasted the school district superintendent.

"It's not fine," said one angry mother. "My kid's in fifth grade, and he barely knows that four and three equalizes nine [*sic*]."

"Yeah!" agreed a father. "And my little girl told me she thought Christopher Columbo [*sic*] discovered boats."

An English gentleman arose from the back of the room and sneered, "I am simply and utterly appalled at the sheer idiocy of what I'm hearing! Why, every last one of you people seems completely maroonic [*sic*]!"

On those (hopefully) very rare occasions when you want or need to use parentheses within parentheses, use brackets instead:

Although I really like going to the movies (I'm a big fan of detective movies [especially the ones starring that famous guy from the forties who always wore a hat and a pencil mustache and who talked funny]), I never go, because no one ever wants to go with me.

The werewolf (who is really just a nice guy named Tom

[who was a nice guy, anyway, until that bizarre and fateful night long ago]) decided that enough was enough: He was going to eat the neighbor's dachshund.

Use brackets to enclose stage directions:

ANGELA [trying to tie her long hair into a bow beneath her neck]: I think this'll look cute.

JOSEPH [biting on a ruler]: No, it won't, Angela. You'll look insane.

ANGELA [continuing in her efforts]: No, I won't. I'll look adorable.

JOSEPH [throwing the ruler across the room, standing]: No, Angela! No! No woman wears her own hair as a giant bow tie! Stop it! Stop it!

ANGELA [pulling both sides of her hair-bow as she finishes]: There. Now doesn't this look cute? And see how my hair's framing my face?

JOSEPH [lunging at her]: I hate you! I hate you and your stupid hair! I can't stand it anymore! [As he knocks over the couch she's on, they both disappear from sight. Curtain.]

And now you can hack it in the bracket racket.

CHAPTER 12
THE HYPHEN

Ah, the hyphen. Small, but mighty. Cute, but powerful. Perky, yet resolute. Staid, yet winsomely sassy.

Is it any wonder that during her acceptance speech for the special Oscar awarded her in 1934 by the Academy of Motion Picture Arts and Sciences, little Shirley Temple chirped, ". . . And most of all, I'd like to thank that most wonderful of all the punctuation marks, the hyphen, which I personify! And none of you better ever forget it!"

Okay, fine—she didn't say that. But how surprised would anyone have been if she had? What *don't* Shirley Temple and the hyphen have in common, besides that one's a punctuation mark and the other was "America's Sweetheart" during the Depression, the most successful child actor in the history of Hollywood, who was a star, before she was seven years old, of twenty films that were so wildly popular around the world that they turned 20th Century Fox into a colossal film studio, and who, after her film career, went on to serve four American presidents as a brilliant diplomat and ambassador?

Sure, if you nitpick your way through their résumés, you'll find differences between the hyphen and Shirley Temple Black. (In 1950, Ms. Temple married California businessman Charles Black, to whom she remains happily married to this day. Alas, the hyphen, a capable and inveterate coupler, seems destined forever to remain a matchmaker, but never a matchee.) But in essence they're the same.

When Shirley Temple was a star, she was small.
The hyphen is, well, a smaller version of the dash.
A diplomat brings people together.
A hyphen brings words together.

And both hyphens and diplomats are firmly dedicated to the belief that when people (or words) come together and really *work* together, they can achieve something significantly more powerful than either of them might have achieved alone.

You may or may not choose to become an international diplomat—but you can certainly learn to hyphenate correctly. And the good news is that proper hyphen usage doesn't involve learning multiple languages, or anything about geography, history, sociology, or politics. All you have to know is:

Use hyphens to join some compound words. A compound results when words that usually appear alone are instead joined together by Shirley Temple—er, by a *hyphen*, we mean. The tricky thing about compound words is that there are no hard-and-fast rules about when they're openly styled (e.g., *high school, guilt trip, line dance, rocking chair*), when they're closed styled (e.g., *highbrow, prizefighter, bookcase, spaceship*), or when they're hyphenated (e.g., *man-hour, mother-in-law, tongue-lashing, user-friendly*). The only sure way to know whether it's, say, *manic depressive* or *manic-depressive* (which it is) is to consult a reputable, current dictionary.

As the joke goes: Does *anal retentive* have a hyphen? Gee, I don't know, but it sure has a colon.

Well, if you look in your reputable, current dictionary, you'll find that *anal-retentive* does indeed have a hyphen.

Often, hyphens join two or more words that, taken together, form an adjective. The tin-of-ear among us write *three day shipping* and *eight man crew*. But the clear-eared, hearing no pause between the two or more words that make up the modifier, write *three-day shipping* and *eight-man crew,* as well as *front-office decision, state-of-the-art technology, zero-tolerance approach*, and—well, you get the idea.

The main thing to bear in mind when trying to determine whether it's time to use two separate words or one compound word is the degree to which it would be confusing to use one or the other. That's your basic, down-and-dirty hyphenation rule: Do whatever makes the sentence make sense.

Are you selling two acre lots, or two-acre lots? Do you wish to purchase six-foot-long rods, or six foot-long rods?

Did you see your boss from work go into a dirty movie theater, or a dirty-movie theater? Did you see a man eating lobster, or a man-eating lobster? Are you a high speed freak, or a high-speed freak?

What do you make of this real-life statement printed on a wedge of Ouray cheese?:

> Ripened cheese from grass fed Guernsey and Jersey cows.

Is the cheese made from grass that was fed cows? Well-placed hyphens would avoid the ambiguity:

> Ripened cheese from grass-fed Guernsey and Jersey cows.

So you can see how it sometimes matters very much whether you hyphenate or not—and how the intended meaning of the words should tell you one way or another.

In words consisting of a prefix and a root, use a hyphen if *not* using one will cause to run together either two vowels or a small letter and a capital:

anti-inflammatory   un-American
extra-alkaline   pre-Christian

Use a hyphen to spell out numbers from twenty-one to ninety-nine:

twenty-five   thirty-three   ninety-six

Use a hyphen to divide a word at the end of a line of text.

Easy enough, except be sure *never* to divide a one-syllable word, even if it ends in *-ed*. If it's one syllable, move the whole (little) word to the next line. When in doubt about exactly where one syllable ends and the next begins, turn once again to your trusty old pal, Dick Shinary.

Dick Shinary will also help you to avoid breaking a word at an awkward or confusing juncture. We recently did a double take when we read the following sentence in our local sports section:

> Parker, a New York Gi-
> ants defensive end, was rear-
> rested this week in connec-
> tion with the death of his
> girlfriend's 4-year-old son.

Rear-rested for *rearrested*? Clearly the product of a typeset-ting program run amok. Until these computer programs become more sophisticated or newspaper editors commit themselves to correcting the havoc their machines have wreaked, we readers will continue to chuckle at or sigh about unintentionally loopy hyphenation. Have a look at some more genuine, authentic, cer-tified, they-really-happened hyphos (a word we've made up on the model of *typos*): *sung-lasses, barf-lies, warp-lanes, doork-nobs, brooms-ticks, pre-gnant, airs-trips, boots-traps, stars-truck, sli-pup,* and *ong-oing.*

Here are some hyphos that we've made up. In each state-ment, assume that the hyphen comes at the end of a line:

The canteen was dedicated to serv-icemen.
The veterinarian treated the tiger by inserting a cat-heter.
A history of the Middle Ages will appear on wee-knights.
Computers will one day enter their dot-age.
Her tight dress caused her to become embarr-assed.
The careless dragon burnt its-elf.
To relieve her mental anguish, she sought help from the-
    rapists.
The all-girl orchestra was a bit weak in the bras-s section.

But seriously, gentle reader. Knowing how to hyphenate properly means, of course, that you're now faced with the decision of whether or not to take the next logical step and become an international diplomat. The important thing is to remember that no matter what you do with your life, if you want to do something *big* with it, you'll do well to remember the example of Shirley Temple Black-hyphen, and start small.

CHAPTER 13
THE ELLIPSIS

Whenever you hear the word *ellipsis,* what's the first thing that comes to your mind—after *Why is this boring person talking to me?* Well, when you hear the word *ellipsis,* you probably think of one celestial body being covered up by another. But that's an eclipse. An ellipsis and eclipse are two different things. An ellipsis represents something that isn't there but is supposed to be. An eclipse happens when something is there that's *not* supposed to be.

So you wouldn't want to mix those up.

What's also confusing about the word *ellipsis* is that it sounds like it should refer to more than one thing. But it's a single punctuation mark, made of three repeating punctuation marks—any one of which, if used alone, would be an entirely *different* punctuation mark. So you can see there's nothing confusing about that at all.

And to be absolutely certain that you remain crystal clear on this gem of a mark, train yourself never, ever to think of an ellipsis without simultaneously thinking of the Andrews Sisters.

Not the three witches in Macbeth.

Not the Three Musketeers.

Not the Three Bears, the Three Little Pigs, or the Three Blind Mice.

And certainly not the Three Stooges.

Forget the Three Stooges. That's just too immature.

Go with the Andrews Sisters. Like the points in an ellipsis there are three of them, and they work seamlessly as one. And . . . um . . . if all their hair fell out and you looked at them from above, they'd kind of look like an ellipsis.

(Oh: For those of you too young to know, the three Andrews Sisters were an American smash-hit singing sensation during the time of World War II, a war fought in the early 1940s that involved a lot of the world [and it wasn't the first time, either]. The Andrews Sisters—LaVerne, Maxene, and Patty—sang harmonies so wondrously smooth, fast, and tight it was like listening to angels on speed. Their biggest hit was "Boogie Woogie Bugle Boy." Check out the names of some of their other blockbusters: "Scrub Me, Mama, with a Boogie Beat"; "Bounce Me, Brother, with a Solid Four"; and "Beat Me, Daddy, Eight to the Bar." So they were actually kind of scary.)

And just as the Andrews Sisters had to follow certain rules (keep hair coiffed; don't topple off insanely high heels; easy on the cleavage; no dress length above the knees; no burping during songs), the ellipsis has certain rules that it must obey, too:

•   •   • **Use an ellipsis to indicate the intentional omission of one or more words within a sentence:**

For he's a jolly good fellow . . . which nobody can deny!

. . . and that's when I realized Irene was probably a cannibal.

His police car radio was filled with static, so all that Detective Joe Friday could gather from the emergency all-points bulletin was "All citizens should be on the lookout for a man approximately . . . of age, last seen wearing a green . . . and driving a . . . missing one wheel. Suspect is described as being . . . tall and having . . . hair . . . and . . . eyes. Suspect is considered extremely dangerous, and should not under any circumstances . . . cherry Slurpee."

The Camp Hackawackaway employee manual is explicit on the matter: ". . . notwithstanding that camp should be an enjoyable experience for all, under no circumstances should counselors, staff, or any other representative of Camp Hackawackaway continue in the erroneous belief that it's somehow humorous to hide all the children in the woods during Parents' Visiting Day."

Note that there's always a space before and after the ellipsis as well as between the periods that make up the ellipsis. The only exception is that the Punctuation Gods have decreed that four-dot ellipsis (discussed on page 123) are never preceded by a space.

● ● ● **Use an ellipsis to indicate that a list goes on beyond those items actually spelled out in the text:**

An evil witch, a tap-dancing scarecrow, flying monkeys, an emotionally unstable lion, disturbing Munchkins . . .

Dorothy couldn't help but wonder if, in the wonderful Land of Oz, they sold guns.

Eggshells, bacon, bits of tissue paper, chocolate chips . . . Belinda's hand flew to her mouth as she spied on her mother-in-law stuffing the Thanksgiving turkey.

We wouldn't call you an idiot, but. . . . [Yep, there's an extra dot in this one, and we'll explain that later.]

• • • **You can use an ellipsis to indicate a hesitation in someone's speaking:**

"Mom, Dad," said Snow White. "I'd like you to meet my roommates—Doc, Grumpy, Sneezy, Dopey . . . Dorky . . . Rudolph. . . . Well, anyway, they all live here."

"Nobody move!" screamed the bank robber. "Everybody pull out your wallets! Wait . . . I don't care about your wallets: This is a bank. Duh. Okay, everybody just stand over against this wall here . . . except then everybody outside can see you. Um, let's see . . . okay, everybody . . . I don't know. . . . Say, am I the only one in here who could really go for a burger?"

• • • **When an ellipsis occurs within the sentence, use just the three points. But when punctuation is needed to clarify the meaning or sense of the original quoted material, appropriate punctuation can go on either side of the ellipsis:**

Tank addressed his impassioned speech to his giant

stuffed bear Sniffles, his poster of Shania Twain, his pet iguana, the ball he'd made from the hair of different dogs . . . "From now on," he declared, "things are going to be different around here!"

"Oh fie, fie! . . . ," cried Bartholomew, who everyone agreed was definitely born in the wrong century.

● ● ● **An ellipsis should consist of four dots when the omission ends a sentence or falls between sentences:**

"I cannot believe that you are daring to suggest some relationship between your missing money and my bulging pockets. . . ." [Here the omitted material comes after *pockets,* and the last dot is the period.]

An out-of-print textbook on the history of architecture sheds some light on the matter: "During the Renaissance, men inexplicably began stuffing outsized, upward-curving protuberances into the front of their leggings. . . . A 1672 legal case (*Women of Pisa vs. Every Stupid Man in This Stupid Town*) rendered the wearing of codpieces illegal (and laid the foundation for later truth-in-advertising laws). Piqued by this censure, the leading men of the area banded together, and almost overnight invented architecture. . . . And that is how we got the Leaning Tower of Pisa." [In both occurrences, the first dot (note the lack of spacing before it) is the period, and the remaining three are the ellipsis.]

Hey, we don't want to say that you're now a genius with ellipsis, but. . . .

AFTERWORD

Thanks so much for reading our little book. If *Comma Sense* was half the fun to read that it was to write, please accept our apologies for the cramps now paralyzing your face. We feel your pain.

Having finished this book makes you an official Grand Poobah and Passionate Pasha of Punctuation. Yay! And this, of course, means that you are now likely to begin writing a good deal more often and more confidently than you used to. Yay and yay again! There are far too few writers these days (although we understand how unlikely it is that you share that sentiment if you happen to be reading this in one of those ten-acre megabookstores).

Write on, we say! Write away! Have at it!—Letters! Memos! Post-its! E-mails! Essays! Stories! Ransom notes! Wait. Scratch that last one, please: Always use your ability to punctuate properly for good, not for evil. After all, you don't want to wind up like Batman's archnemesis, The Riddler, do you? Remember how that quintessentially querulous querier ended up wearing giant question marks plastered all over his, um, body-tard? All right, then.

One of the very best ways to employ your newfound punctuational prowess is to write to us: Rich (a.k.a. Attila the Pun, Conan the Grammarian, the Viceroy of Verbivores) is always happy to take a moment away from his prodigious authoring and lecturing to respond to an inquiry or comment. And John (a.k.a. Hey You, Mr. Shore, The Giant Who Feeds Us) is always happy to take a moment away from his prodigious . . . well, couch-sitting and cat-petting to do the same.

Rich can be reached at: richard.lederer@pobox.com

John is at: johnshore@sbcglobal.net

And now, partner in punctuation, the time has come for us to tip our hats, point our trusty steeds westward, and, with our heads held high, go writing off into the sunset.

CHEAT SHEET

As a kind of super-duper, handy-dandy, razzle-dazzle cheat sheet for punctuation mastery, we offer a compact lineup of the rules that are scattered throughout this book. Here we present the marks in alphabetical order. Each rule also lists the page or pages of the book where it's discussed more fully, if you feel you need additional information or explanation.

The Apostrophe

To grant possession to a singular noun, simply add an apostrophe and _s_ (page 67):

The student's love of punctuation is boundless.

If a plural noun that already ends in _s_ needs to become possessive, slap a single apostrophe on the end of that word (pages 68–71):

The students' love of punctuation is boundless.

To form the possessive of plural nouns that don't end in s, add an apostrophe and s (page 71):

The men's love of punctuation is boundless.

If two or more people possess the same thing, you need only put the apostrophe after the last one of the two mentioned (page 72):

Len and Barry's seminar teaches a love of punctuation.

If two people own items individually, you must show your respect by giving them each an 's (page 73):

Len's and Barry's wives love punctuation.

The possessive form of it is spelled its (page 74):

The level of a civilization is measured by the precision of its punctuation.

Apostrophes mark the omission of one or more letters in common contractions (pages 75–76):

It's a good thing to love punctuation.

Avoid gratuitous apostrophes for plurals and bogus present-tense markers (pages 76–77):

Don't write the likes of "Even little boy's and girl's love punctuation."

The apostrophe indicates the omission of elements in a word or number (page 79):

At exactly twelve o'clock midnight, way back in '02, I started to love punctuation.

The apostrophe forms plurals of letters and words whenever the absence of an apostrophe would be confusing (page 80):

I love mastering the do's and don'ts of punctuation.

But where there is no confusion, don't use apostrophes to form plurals (page 80):

Sometime in the 1990s, I started to love punctuation.

Add an apostrophe and *s* after words and names ending in *s, z*, and *x* sounds if you would pronounce the *'s* in that word or name (pages 81):

The boss's daughter loves punctuation, but all of Achilles' descendants do not.

Brackets

Within a quotation, use brackets to insert a missing or explanatory word or comment (page 105):

He told the reporters, "I [love] punctuation."

Use brackets around the italicized word *sic* (from Latin, meaning "thus," or "thus it is," or "that's the way the cookie actually crumbled") to indicate that an error or peculiarity in a quotation is being reproduced exactly as it was originally said or written (pages 105–6):

"I love funktuation [sic]!" exulted the student.

On those very rare occasions when you want or need to use parentheses within parentheses, use brackets instead (pages 106–7):

I love punctuation (although I'm a bigger fan of spelling [more specifically spelling reform]), particularly the gorgeous curves of the question mark.

Brackets are commonly used to enclose stage directions (page 107):

> ANGELA [trying to tie her long hair into a bow beneath her neck]:
> I love punctuation.

The Colon

Use a colon to introduce just about anything: a quotation, a list, a complete statement, or the very words you are reading right now—anything that explains or expands upon the part of the sentence it immediately follows (which is almost always an independent clause). In other words, what comes *after* a colon delivers on the promise set up by what comes *before* it (pages 51–52):

> I never met a punctuation mark I didn't love: apostrophes, brackets, colons, commas, ellipsis points, and so on.

Capitalize an independent clause that follows a colon. Anything else, don't (page 52):

> I love punctuation: My tennis partner is a parenthesis, and I sleep with a doll in the form of an exclamation point.

Use a colon—never a semicolon, please!—after the opening salutation of a formal letter (page 53):

> Dear Reader:
> I love punctuation.

Use a comma instead of a colon after the "Dear (insert name here)" part when the letter is casual or informal (page 53):

> Dear Meathead,
> I love punctuation.

Place a colon between hours and minutes in expressing time (page 53):

I love punctuation from 12:12 p.m. to 7:77 a.m.

Place a colon between titles and subtitles of books and articles (page 53–54):

I Love Punctuation: Confessions of a Correctness Addict

Between the names of characters and their lines in a play or movie (page 54):

SIR REGINALD: I love punctuation.

LADY THISTLEBOTTOM: So do I, and much more than I love you.

Between chapters and verses in the Bible (page 54):

In Psalms 15:22, we read, "The love of punctuation is the root of all rectitude."

Colons are used in ratios (page 54):

The ratio between my love of punctuation and my love of chocolate is 100:1.

The Comma

Use commas to separate words, phrases, or clauses in a series (pages 28–30):

I love punctuation, grammar, and spelling.

Use commas to list adjectives in a series if the adjectives are of equal importance (page 30):

I love the elegant, sophisticated, intricate aspects of punctuation.

Do not use commas to list adjectives in a series if the adjectives seem so closely related as to form a single unit (page 30):

I own a thick college textbook about punctuation.

Use commas before coordinating conjunctions (*and, but, for, nor, or, so, yet*) to join two independent clauses (pages 30–33):

I love punctuation, but I hate parsing sentences.

Use commas to set off introductory elements (pages 33–35):

To be honest, I love punctuation.

When elements come in the middle or the end of a sentence and you hear a strong pause before and afterward, set them off with commas (pages 35–36):

I love punctuation, baby, and I respect everybody else who shares that love.

Use commas to set off nonrestrictive clauses (pages 36–37):

Throckmorton Turlington, who is my best friend, loves punctuation.

Do not use commas to set off a restrictive clause (pages 36–37):

People who love punctuation live longer.

Use commas to set off complete quotations (page 37):

The great general George S. Patton once said, "I love punctuation."

Use commas to set off the year from the day of the month, and the state from the city (pages 37–38):

March 21, 1958, is a day set aside by the citizens of Lynchburg, Tennessee, to express their love of punctuation.

Employ a comma whenever using one will prevent confusion (page 38):

Hemingway did not, like Fitzgerald, love punctuation.

The Dash

Use dashes in pairs to set off a thought or explanatory remark within a sentence (page 59):

Although I love punctuation—I've been married to all three ellipsis points—I found true happiness with an umlaut.

Dashes are one choice you have to introduce an appositive (a noun or noun cluster that elaborates on the noun that comes before it) (pages 59–60):

I love the umlaut for one reason—its utter lack of diacritical remarks.

You can use a dash to signify a sudden change in thought (page 60):

Punctuation loves me; punctuation loves me not; punctuation loves me; punctuation loves me not—then again, what am I doing asking the opinion of a flower?

Use a dash before the citation of an author or source of a quotation (page 61):

"He who loves punctuation loves life."—Richard Lederer and John Shore

The Ellipsis

Use an ellipsis to indicate the intentional omission of one or more words within a sentence (pages 120–21):

For he's a jolly good punctuator . . . which nobody can deny!

Use an ellipsis to indicate that a statement goes on beyond those items actually spelled out in the text (pages 121–22):

I wouldn't say that I love punctuation, but. . . .

You can use ellipsis to indicate a hesitation in someone's speaking (page 122):

"Mother, I love punctuation!" screamed Principal Skinner. "I love those little dots! Wait . . . I don't care about dots. . . . Okay, Mother, I love . . . straight lines! Um . . . I guess I love those little curvy squiggles most of all!"

When an ellipsis occurs within the sentence, use just the three points. But when punctuation is needed to clarify the meaning or sense of the original quoted material, appropriate punctuation can go on either side of the ellipsis (pages 122–23):

"I wouldn't say that I love punctuation, but . . . ," winked Lucretia.

An ellipsis should consist of four dots when the omission ends a sentence or falls between sentences (page 123):

"I wouldn't say that I love punctuation, but. . . ."

The Exclamation Point

Use the exclamation point to emphasize an emotion or put starch into a command (pages 20–22):

I love punctuation!

The Hyphen

Use hyphens to join some compound words (pages 112–14):
I love punctuation more than I love a three-tiered sundae.

In words consisting of a prefix and a root, use a hyphen if not using one will cause to run together either two vowels or a small letter and a capital (page 114):
I love punctuation because it's anti-inflationary.

Use a hyphen to spell out numbers from twenty-one to ninety-nine (page 114):
If I've told you once, I've told you ninety-nine times: I love punctuation.

Use a hyphen to divide a word at the end of a line of text (pages 114–16):
If I've told you once, I've told you ninety-nine times: I love punctuation because it's anti-inflationary.

Parentheses

Use parentheses to set off comments and explanations that are not closely connected to the rest of the sentence (pages 98–100):
I (actually we—Richard Lederer and John Shore) love (and we do mean love) punctuation.

When you write a parenthesized statement as a freestanding sentence, follow the same capitalization and punctuation rules you would for any sentence (page 100):

I love punctuation. (Doesn't everybody?)

Use parentheses to enclose numbers or letters introducing items in a series that are part of a running text. Use parentheses in pairs; a parenthesis looks lonely by itself (page 100):

I love punctuation because it's (1) elegant, (2) slimming, (3) cholesterol-reducing, and (4) anti-inflationary.

The Period

A period marks the conclusion of any sentence that doesn't end with an exclamation point or a question mark (page 6):

I love punctuation.

In U.S. punctuation, periods always go inside the quotation marks (pages 6, 91):

Samantha explained, "I love punctuation."

Periods belong inside parentheses that enclose a freestanding sentence and outside parentheses that enclose material that is not a full statement (page 7):

I love punctuation. (Anybody who cares about civilization loves it, too.)

I love punctuation (bearing in mind, of course, that everybody else does, too).

Periods are also used in sundry conventional ways; for example, for numbers, abbreviations, and initials (page 7):

Dr. M. T. Handed loves punctuation.

The Question Mark

Place a question mark at the end of a question (pages 14–15):
How do I love punctuation? Let me count the ways.

Quotation Marks

Use quotation marks to set off direct quotations and dialogue. In dialogue, use a new paragraph to indicate a change of speaker (pages 87–88):
"I love punctuation!" I screamed. "I really, really love it."
"Not as much as I love spelling rules," she riposted.

Do not place quotation marks around indirect discourse or paraphrase (page 88):
I said that I love punctuation.

Use single quotation marks to set off a quotation within a quotation (pages 88–89):
"I said to her, 'I love punctuation.'"

Use quotation marks to set off the titles of short works—poems, book chapters, magazine articles, short stories, songs, and the like—that are usually included in longer works. Use italics (underlining on some keyboards) to indicate the titles of longer works—books, anthologies, magazines, record albums, motion pictures, operas, and the like (page 89):
"I Love Punctuation" became the lead article in the August 2005 issue of *Semicolon Fanciers Quarterly*.

Use quotation marks (or italics) to distinguish words-as-words (page 89):

The word "punctuation" derives from two ancient roots: "punc," meaning "a hoodlum," and "tuation," meaning "desire to become."

Or:

The word *punctuation* derives from two ancient roots: *punc,* meaning "a hoodlum," and *tuation,* meaning "desire to become."

Use single quotation marks to set off quoted material that occurs within a quotation (pages 90–91):

The professor explained, "The word 'punctuation' derives from two ancient roots: punc, meaning 'hoodlum,' and tuation, meaning 'desire to become.' "

Don't use quotation marks gratuitously, (page 91), as in:

I "love" punctuation.

In U.S. punctuation, periods and commas always go inside the quotation marks (pages 6, 91):

"I love punctuation," I confessed.

I confessed, "I love punctuation."

Semicolons and colons always go outside the quotation marks (pages 91–92):

I confessed, "I love punctuation"; then I explained, "I also love spelling rules."

"Punctuation": Ah, how that word makes my heart thump.

When question marks and exclamation points compete with commas and periods, question marks and exclamation points take precedence (page 92):

I asked, "Do you think that I love punctuation?"

I exclaimed, "I love punctuation!"

Question marks and exclamation points go either inside or outside of the final quotation marks, depending on whether the question or exclamation is part of the quoted material or expresses the tone of the sentence as a whole (pages 92–93):

I asked, "Do you think that I love punctuation?"

Did you hear me say, "I love punctuation"?

I exclaimed, "I love punctuation!"

How wonderful that I can finally confess, "I love punctuation"!

Here's how you resolve those (hopefully) rare collisions of question marks and exclamation points, with each other and themselves (page 93):

Did you hear me ask, "Do you think that I love punctuation?"

How wonderful that I can exclaim, "I love punctuation!"

Did you hear me exclaim, "I love punctuation!"?

How wonderful that I asked, "Do you think that I love punctuation?"!

The Semicolon

Use a semicolon to join closely related independent clauses (groups of words that could stand on their own as an independent sentence, were they asked to do so) in compound sentences (pages 44–45):

> I love punctuation; I even love spelling rules.

When the second clause is introduced by a conjunctive adverb (*then, however, nevertheless, moreover, thus, therefore,* and the like), use a semicolon (page 45):

> I love punctuation; therefore, I am a good person.

Use a semicolon to separate independent clauses that already contain commas (page 46):

> We, your faithful authors, love punctuation; but we don't join punctuation fan clubs, shop for punctuation action figures, and let our lives revolve around little black marks.

Use a semicolon as an extrapowerful comma between items in a series that already contain commas (page 46):

> Although we have tried to explain in a tasteful, entertaining manner the distinctions among end-of-sentence marks of punctuation, such as periods, question marks, and exclamation points; separating marks, such as commas and semicolons; and introducing marks of punctuation, such as commas, colons, and dashes, you probably still feel that we are two guys who have too much time on our hands.